Old Women Show
Your Arms and
Share Your Stories

Unless otherwise identified, all Scripture quotations in this publication are taken from the *Holy Bible, New International Version*® (NIV®). Copyright © 1973, 1978, 1984, 2011 by Biblica, Inc.® Used by permission of Zondervan. All rights reserved.

Scripture quotations marked (TLB) are taken from *The Living Bible,* copyright © 1971. Used by permission of Tyndale House Publishers, a Division of Tyndale House Ministries, Carol Stream, Illinois 60188. All rights reserved.

Dreamy (5x8) Self-Publishing Template © 2017 Renee Fisher
https://www.reneefisher.com

Cover Design: Nelly Murariu at PixBeeDesign.com

ISBN-13: 978-0-578-70948-2

Old Women Show Your Arms and Share Your Stories

FINDING GOD'S PERSISTENT PRESENCE IN EVERYDAY LIFE

Kim Roberts Mosko

GOD IS PRESENT
PRESS

Dedication

To Victoria and Sophie. You are the light of
my life, and you occupy every space of my
heart with love and fulfillment. I could never
have asked for, or dreamed of, a purpose
with more passion than being your mother.
You provide a love greater than I can contain.
You have left your precious spirit imprints
on my soul, and I love you with every
fiber of my being. May you walk this life
with courage, confidence, and connection
and a reliance on your Creator for all of it.
Remember always, I love you most.

Contents

Foreword

I want to be the kind of Christian that Brennan Manning deems a worthy reader for *The Ragamuffin Gospel*: one of the "smart people who know they are stupid and honest disciples who admit they are scalawags." I know God desires this for me as well, and I am thankful for the hardships He has allowed as they have furthered my "Ragamuffin" journey. May I accept future trials more graciously and faithfully.

Manning proclaimed *The Ragamuffin Gospel* for a specific type of reader. I want to be a part of that audience—a redeemed beneficiary of God's love.

Manning warned his readers that his book was written for:

the bedraggled, beat-up, and burnt-out.

It is for the wobbly and weak-kneed who know they don't have it all together and are too proud to accept the handout of amazing grace.

It is for inconsistent, unsteady disciples whose cheese is falling off their cracker.

It is for poor, weak, sinful men and women with hereditary faults and limited talents.

It is for earthen vessels who shuffle along on feet of clay.

It is for the bent and the bruised who feel that their lives are a grave disappointment to God.

It is for smart people who know they are stupid and honest disciples who admit they are scalawags.

—Brennan Manning, *The Ragamuffin Gospel*

Introduction

T he older I get, the less I want to show my arms. Each year, they lose more and more tone, and they jiggle when I move. Not attractive. But here is what I am learning: The older I get, the more I need to show not only my arms but all my weaknesses. I have finally realized that God uses my shortcomings, mistakes, and hardships to strengthen me and draw me to Him.

Mother Angelica once said, "I'm not afraid to fail. I'm scared to death of dying and having the Lord say to me, 'Angelica, this is what you might have done had you trusted more.'" Well, I, Kim Roberts Mosko, don't want God to ask me why I chose to tell no one how He saved me and really provided for me in some of the most overwhelming moments of life.

In these stories—silly and serious—I want to share with you how His redemptive grace and love rescued me. I want to tell about God's persistent presence in my life and some of the ways He blessed me and taught me about love and character from the extraordinary people He placed in my life. I want to honor Him. I am so grateful for His consistency and for all the times He carried me. Sometimes I was aware of His closeness, and other times I felt alone, but through it all, God answered my prayers (those spoken and those hidden in my heart) and provided me with a path to Him. He was there every day and in every season. His mercy and love will be there for you, too.

I am not suggesting I have arrived. I am a little stubborn and a lot impatient, so God has more work to complete in me.

I still have much to learn and desire to be open to what God has to show me. I want you to have these stories so, as you grow through the seasons of life, you can hear my voice and know my heart. I hope it doesn't sound like advice or as if I am telling you how to do things. Instead, I pray it provides encouragement as you find your way. Know you can handle anything life brings because you have a God who is mightier than all of it and loves you unconditionally.

I think you will see how God showed up for me and how He never actually left in the first place. I want you to be reminded that God:

Is good.

Is in control.

Can be trusted.

My mother lived by these truths. She wrote them prominently in her Bible. She worked faithfully to know God and to actively engage with and trust Him. I have included some of her wisdom I found in the notes she wrote in her Bible. What a blessing to have her insights from the verses she loved most.

These stories are for my daughters, Victoria and Sophie. I love you both more than you will ever know, and my prayer is that you will seek God and trust His presence as you travel this pilgrimage called life.

These stories are also for you, dear reader. There is room for more daughters and more mothers to listen in. May you be encouraged by these short vignettes of God's grace, love, and persistent presence.

ONE

On Motherhood

The Greatest of Blessings from God and a Glimpse into His Heart for Me

My husband often joked that I did not make a good pregnant person. My face was puffy, my ankles were swollen, and my sweet and salty cravings were insatiable. My changing and uncomfortable physical state could have certainly led one to conclude pregnancy was not for me. Like most things, however, the exterior doesn't always reflect the interior or tell the story of the heart. This was true for me.

Contrary to what one might have concluded, I loved being pregnant. Nothing felt more significant than carrying my daughters in my womb. Knowing they were with me as I greeted each day gave me a sense of purpose like no other. The intense love and fulfillment I felt in pregnancy continued as I watched both of them grow into the unique humans God destined them to become.

Being Mom to Victoria and Sophie has been the greatest joy of my life. It has also given me a glimpse into God's heart for me. I love them unconditionally and with all my soul. There is nothing they could do to divert my love from them. It grows stronger with each phase of their lives. Hasn't the Lord assured us of this unwavering love from Him? "For I am convinced that neither death nor life, neither angels nor demons, neither the present nor the future, nor any powers, neither height nor depth, nor anything else in all creation, will be able to separate us from the love of God that is in Christ Jesus our Lord" (Romans 8:38-39).

I will never forget the way Victoria Lee, my firstborn, looked up at me the first time I held her. It seemed she was telling me it would be okay. It's as if God placed all His reassurance for this new journey with her in her big, beautiful brown eyes. I instantly felt comfortable with her in my arms and hopeful about all of God's plans for her. Victoria's first look at me was a preview of the way she would walk this life. She seems to know everything will be okay despite the uncertainty of any given moment. She has such a robust, willing spirit and will do what it takes to make things happen. She may feel uncomfortable or uneasy, but she has a strong sense of self and the limits she can push. I have watched Victoria carry herself through good and bad times with this mighty confidence. It helps her seek and follow God's path for her life. I have witnessed her ability to change course because her call from God was in another direction. Her keen ability to see life as it is and engage it with humor is a blessing to us all. Her willing, can-do spirit inspires us and will be a gift to her family and a guide for her path.

*The most powerful
and awe-inspiring God
gave them life and will
grow them in His ways.
They may sometimes
resist His wisdom
because its price can
come with pain, but
He desires only good
for them—for all of us.*

Sophie Marie immediately had all of our attention (including the nurses and doctors) the second she was born. Not because she was screaming or moving about, but because she was so still. The nurses rushed to her to ensure no emergency intervention was necessary. Instead, they reported she was not only healthy but strong—such a prelude to how she would live her sweet life. Her quiet confidence demands respect. We all sense her spirituality. I am often amazed at Sophie's ability to see and hear God. It has allowed her to walk a path that draws others to her. God granted her the gift of knowing, and it has provided her with Christlike compassion for others. Her tenacity to do what she needs to do gives me great comfort as her mother. I never worry that she won't figure things out. She always does and always will. I can't wait to see how God will use Sophie's emotional and spiritual depth. No doubt, her family will benefit greatly from these traits.

Writing this story has made me doubt my ability to correctly choose the words that will convey the depths of my love for my daughters. Someone once said having a child is like watching your heart walk outside of your body. This accurately describes the sensation but omits the deep longing I have to protect this heart—my daughters—at all costs and never witness its angst.

I have learned, however, I must let them walk this life as it comes. I cannot stop heartache from greeting them or occasionally tackling them to the ground. I can pray they will feel their angels, the ones God blessed them with at birth, and know that He is their protector. The most powerful and awe-inspiring God gave them life and will grow them in

His ways. They may sometimes resist His wisdom because its price can come with pain, but He desires only good for them—for all of us. He granted both of my girls unique gifts to thrive in this life. As they let God use them for His good, they and their families will find fulfillment.

Thank you, God, for the blessing of motherhood and for entrusting me with the precious souls of Victoria and Sophie. May they know my deep and everlasting love for them. With all my heart and soul, Lord, I humbly petition all Your graces for them.

"'Real isn't how you are made,' said the Skin Horse. 'It's a thing that happens to you. When a child loves you for a long, long time, not just to play with, but REALLY loves you, then you become Real.'"

—Margery Williams, *The Velveteen Rabbit*

"May you learn to laugh together and cry together as you share each other's joys and pains. May you hold high each other's strengths and minimize each other's weaknesses."

—Nancy Roberts' inscription in *Mothers and Daughters*
by Lauren Cowen and Jayne Wexler

"May you take delight in each other's triumphs and show empathy in each other's defeats."

—Nancy Roberts' inscription in *Mothers and Daughters*
by Lauren Cowen and Jayne Wexler

TWO

Nono and Her Legacy

How We Were Blessed with Unconditional Love and a Path to Holiness Through One Woman's Yes to God

How can a story about the person I admire most on Earth be so hard to write? I think it is because I want to cover it all—her undying and unconditional love for family, her ability to care for others, and her never-ending obedience to God. Traits usually associated with saints. No doubt, she was close to God, and her gift for loving others gave her a likeness to Him I have never again observed.

There are so many ways my sweet mom, "Nono" to her grandchildren, demonstrated this likeness. I could go on and on about the lives she touched in her family, as well as the students she taught and the people she walked with during troubled times. My daughters know a lot of those stories and were blessed to experience her uniqueness in their own lives.

I think the holiest part of her journey, however, was her consistent yes to God. It provided her a sense of peace and joy that I hope one day to obtain. It's not easy to say yes to God when the lights on the road have dimmed, and the path you must walk holds a detour. Yet, Nono had a faith that allowed her to trust God even when the unmapped road was precisely where she found herself.

Uncertain about her future and frightened about what would come, Nono said yes to God when my dad received a fatal diagnosis. He was just 30 years old when he was told he had polycystic kidney disease and would live to be only 40. That was ten short years. Too few years to watch his children graduate from high school or grow old with his beloved wife. Can you imagine the fear and heartbreak Nono must have felt knowing she would soon lose the love of her life? It must have been overwhelming. She was undoubtedly scared and unsettled about what living without my dad would look like. Nonetheless, she said yes to God and willingly leaned into their precarious path.

Her yes was personified by the joy she exuded. She went back to school and loved learning and, eventually, teaching. She had friends, threw parties, and taught Bible classes on Sunday. For all practical purposes, she carried on as if they would live forever—no worries at all. That was her yes to God. With my father's health in God's hands, Nono could focus on her faith, family, and friends, with a lighthearted spirit that became her trademark. Despite my dad's diagnosis, she gave freely to others and championed many in need. By saying yes to God, she was vowing to live life to the fullest as she trusted the rest to Him.

*The fruit of Nono's
faith and obedience
was a joyful life.
I pray I can follow
her example as I face
life's trials. May I, too,
say yes to God and live
in the completeness
of His hope.*

Another defining yes came again with my father's illness. The disease finally tackled him to the ground, and he spent several years on dialysis in a weakened state. He eventually underwent surgery for a kidney transplant, which left him in the hospital for months fighting one infection after another. He had good days and bad days. Some filled with hope and some with the despair of his prognosis. My mom's yes to God showed in her perseverance to stay relentlessly by my father as he battled to beat the odds. Although she practically lived at the hospital with no life or self-care of her own, she continued to maintain a spirit of peace and joy. Again, she chose to trust God. This complete faith in the Holy Father allowed her to light the hospital halls with her beautiful smile and provide support to my dad like none other.

The infections finally conquered my father's body, and he passed from this life on September 26, 1992. I will never forget Nono's composure when she gave me the news. She looked at me with both weakness and strength as she told me the hour had come. The Lord had called my sweet dad home. Her yes to God had ended with a goodbye to the love of her life. Although her joyful way of living did not result in his victory over death, she continued to trust, hold gratitude, and say yes to God for the remaining years of her life.

This is the story of a woman who blessed us with her unconditional love and zest for life. It is also a prayer of thanksgiving to God for allowing us to witness a woman who sought Him always. A woman whose pursuit of God resulted in her undying love and concern for others. A matriarch who not only captured our love but the love of so many. How blessed we are to have seen firsthand the heart of God working through an ordinary, everyday woman who happened to be our mother, grandmother, and friend.

The fruit of Nono's faith and obedience was a joyful life. Her heart was filled with trust in God's protection over her. Because of that profound faith and resulting joy, not many knew of her troubles. She had turned those over to God. Her dependence and trust in Him gave her the freedom that eludes so many. I pray I can follow her example as I face life's trials. May I, too, say yes to God and live in the completeness of His hope.

Thank you, God, that this is the story I am
honored to tell about the woman I call Mom.
She was my best friend, mentor, and confidant.
It's a story of peace and hope because she loved
and trusted You first.

"Some people care too much. I think it's called love."

—A. A. Milne, *Winnie-the-Pooh*

Mother Teresa had three rules for the spirit of her sisters: 1) loving trust 2) total surrender 3) cheerfulness. Mother Teresa believed cheerfulness was a net with which we can catch souls. I believe Nono's net was mighty and strong as she lived life cheerfully despite her circumstances.

Nono's wisdom: Next to Matthew 6:34 she wrote, "He will take care of me." Nono deeply believed this, and it allowed her to live her life abundantly. May I follow her example and trust God's Word is speaking to me. I must insert my name in Scripture as I proclaim God's providence over me. "So, [Kim/Stew/Victoria/Sophie], don't be anxious about tomorrow. God will take care of your tomorrow too."

(Matthew 6:34, TLB)

THREE

Word of the Year

A New Kind of Resolution

I'm not big on New Year's resolutions. In fact, I have never announced I am officially starting or stopping anything just because a new year was upon me. I dread the feeling of defeat that will undoubtedly arise in February or March when I can no longer maintain my new routine.

Considering my angst around new beginnings, you can imagine my surprise as I listened with intrigue to my dear friend describe her word for the year. I mean, a word might be something I could really get behind. It sounds more thoughtful than a New Year's resolution. This was my kind of movement.

I became more and more enamored as she explained her word and how God revealed it to her. She provided examples of how the meaning in this word might be used to build trust with God over the upcoming year. She described how she could already see it at work in the very first month.

As she talked about the importance of her word, *release*, I began to sense a real connection between her comfort with God and His sovereignty in her word for the year. I detected that the Holy Spirit had laid this word upon her, and she was trusting it would provide her grounding as the year ahead unfolded. This got me thinking and excited about all the possibilities in a word for myself. In fact, as she explained how she would call upon God to help her "release" things to Him, I was convinced this was my word as well. I could not think of a better word, and I proclaimed it as my own.

Over the next few days, God would have some critical input on my word for this year. He must have thought, *If she is actually going to choose a word, I should guide her to one of benefit*. Not knowing God had a different word for me, I began testing the validity of "release." The more I tried out this word, the more I sensed something was missing. Don't get me wrong, releasing my fears, troubles, and all of it to God is always a good thing. It's something I strive for. I just wasn't feeling the connection. I was starting to think this word of the year idea might be a wicked twist on a new year's resolution, and it just wasn't for me.

I nonetheless stayed open over the next several days to see where this word thing might take me. I'm glad I decided to wait, because God made it abundantly clear. Through a mass I attended (where I was convinced the sole purpose of the sermon was to convey my word to me) and some readings I encountered, I was guided to my word—*present*. God was asking me to be present this year. It wasn't the word I had chosen, but it was the word I needed. I was ready for this word. I love being present with people and listening to their stories. It is such a privilege to be there when someone shares their heart. This was a word I could master and one I already loved practicing.

I would soon learn, however, that God was asking me to go deeper. I could sense He was calling me to something that would require a lot of faith in Him. He wanted me to *release* my past and future to Him and focus on the *present*. Could I let go of past sufferings? Would I be able to give Him control so I might enjoy today and remain unconcerned about tomorrow? To live this word, I would have to reside in today. Not the cakewalk I had imagined. It's easy to say I trust God and His plans for me, but my actions often show otherwise. I find it easy to talk about faith but more challenging to walk it. Living in the present would mean trusting God and acknowledging He can see what I cannot.

Mother Angelica, a nun who founded the Eternal Word Television Network, encouraged the faithful to practice "present" living. "Give me this day my daily bread" was her mantra for doing life. I am a Mother Angelica fan, and I have always admired her trust. I assumed her courage to stay present was a gift meant for saints, but not something I would be able to achieve. Well, I am no saint, and yet God was asking me to look no further than today. I would need His help.

I was feeling a tinge of panic. This was going to take some intentionality on my part. First and foremost, I would have to let go of past hardships and accept the lessons they provided. After all, they allowed me to grow. Although I thought I would never emerge from all the struggles, here I stand stronger and more refined. Definitely more dependent on and trusting of God. Now it's time to stop regretting the trials and to start proclaiming the victory. God is asking me to finally accept those tests as I grasp hold of His word *present*.

*Living in the present
would mean trusting God
and acknowledging He
can see what I cannot.*

*As I accept and bid
farewell to past trials,
I must also stop fearing
future ones.*

As I accept and bid farewell to past trials, I must also stop fearing future ones. They will surely come, but I can trust. The mountains I have scaled gave me a greater understanding of who God is as I witnessed His presence. Have I not been the recipient of God's healing and the valuable resources He placed on my path? Didn't He carry me when the climb was too steep and the air too thin? The answer is yes, so my action is to trust. He will be there again. I am free to stop feverishly calculating the future and what I must do to control it. I can give it to Him so I might live fully present in today.

It's only February. Might I throw my arms in the air and proclaim my word is somehow flawed? Possibly. I mean, why should a word last longer than a resolution? But I believe it's inspired by God. Either you believe His providence, or you don't. He has called me to be present in the word He revealed. I trust I need this, and I am choosing this year to let God bless my past and hold the future. I will enjoy today.

God has uniquely provided us with the gift of language. What better way to connect with Him than to focus on a word He gives? I am quickly becoming a complete fan of this new type of resolution as I am looking to God and asking Him to provide me with focus. As I ground myself in His revealed word, I will practice faith in Him. I need the joy of today, not the worry of tomorrow.

Thank You, God, for providing a path. I can't wait to see how this word might offer one avenue of grounding, strength, and comfort through a year of daily connection to You.

"What day is it?" asked Pooh. "It's today," squeaked Piglet. "My favorite day," said Pooh.

—A. A. Milne, *Adventures of Winnie the Pooh*

"The most important and most fruitful acts of our freedom are not those by which we transform the outside world as those by which we change our inner attitude in light of the faith that God can bring good out of everything without exception."

—Jacques Philippe, *Interior Freedom*

"My attitude is, if the Lord inspires me to do something, I attempt to do it. I start and it goes like a snowball downhill. I have to start: if it's not His will, it will either fall apart or something will happen to really hinder it."

—Mother Angelica

FOUR

My Annual Exam

A New Year of Hope and Possibilities

I might be unique in that I don't mind my annual physical exam. It feels a bit like the new year to me: a hint of anticipation overlaid with the possibility of hope. I mean, nothing but possibilities lie ahead when your doctor reports your vitals are good, your blood work is within range, and she will see you next year. This good news always causes me to sigh and offer a quick prayer of thanksgiving.

This year's report from the doctor would not provide such a clear path to a new year. When the nurse called with the lab results, nothing seemed alarming, including the fact that one specific ratio was out of range and would need retesting. This news seemed rather benign, considering all the other blood work revealed normal ranges. I would soon learn from the doctor, however, that unless this ratio fell within range on retesting, I would be referred to an oncologist.

After eight weeks of anticipation, I made my way to the clinic to provide another blood sample. Then I waited. Good news (or so it seemed) as the nurse informed me the concerning ratio had dropped down from its previous high level. A sigh of relief. Unfortunately, the nurse went on to inform me I was being referred to the oncologist. While the number was lower, it was still outside the acceptable norm.

I have never written a story while still living its reality. I want to be honest with you about my emotions as I head to the lab for more blood work, wait for the results, and then meet with the oncologists. In some ways, I have never felt more present (perfect timing on my word for the year). I must admit, part of my peace comes from my lack of worry. While one of the ratios is out of normal range, I don't have any other symptoms, and I feel perfectly fine. Nothing but the blood work indicates a problem. Another part of my calm, however, is grounded in a tremendous sense of God. I physically feel a comfort I cannot explain. It's not unlike the feeling I had after Nono fell and was left in a coma. I remember sensing a heaviness in her room that felt peaceful, as if someone other than me was in complete control. I'm not suggesting the situations are similar. I am not at death's door and may soon learn there is no cause for alarm. I nonetheless sense a profound presence and protection offering me peace around this situation.

I don't want to sound dramatic, and I am not trying to create an exciting read. My motivation is simple. I am writing these stories so you can hear my voice and know my heart. What better way than to share with you this current situation and the peace I feel while waiting in the unknown?

I must admit, it's a kind of peace which could easily elude me. I could quickly turn to my overdrive mode and race to the "what if" questions. I could be examining every possible downside and trying to figure out how to control each situation—a response I have had a lot of practice at implementing. Instead, I am walking through this process as it comes, which is a surprise to me and a gift from God. He is allowing me this grace and the ability to lean into His truth.

By the time you read this story, I will know the results of the retesting and will have met with the oncologist. It is my prayer that there will be nothing further to report, and the blood work scare will have been a fluke. It is also my prayer that I will be able to remain in this place of peaceful presence and trust in Him no matter what the doctor reports. Either way, God is once again using a life event to remind me He is near, and if I am listening, I can tap into His abundant resources of peace, comfort, and protection.

I have no doubt previous life events have given me practice in sensing God. Many times, it took fear and even tears to see He was there. I hope all that practice carries me now. I am intensely aware of how human I am. Can I stay in this place of calm? Will I unravel with unwelcome news? There lies the catch. I am less worried about hearing from the doctor than I am about my ability to remain present. I must counter this fear with gratitude for my current state of peace.

God has brought me here, and He can carry me. He most certainly has allowed me to witness His enormous graces many times before.

I pray I can successfully mark this feeling of God's nearness on my heart. I want to recognize it the next time

I am walking through this
process as it comes, which is
a surprise to me and a gift
from God. He is allowing me
this grace and the ability to
lean into His truth.

God is once again using a
life event to remind me He is
near, and if I am listening,
I can tap into His abundant
resources of peace, comfort,
and protection.

fear attempts to dominate a situation. I may even need to draw more deeply on it as this set of circumstances unfolds. I encourage you to do the same. Take God in through all of your senses so your body will hold His memory and recognize His nearness, and you will be able to access His comfort when you need it most. He gives Himself freely and His comfort is abundant. If you faithfully mark God's presence in your life, your body and heart will recognize His providence the next time He is near. How blessed we are to have a God so deeply concerned with our comfort.

Thank You, God, for helping me to sense Your presence. I pray I will never forget Your comfort and care as I enter new terrain.

"God keeps the entire Universe in order, and still finds time to take a personal interest in you and me."

—Mother Angelica

"God has not been trying an experiment on my faith or love in order to find out their quality. He knew it already. It was I who didn't. In this trial He makes us occupy the dock, the witness box, and the bench all at once. He always knew that my temple was a house of cards. His only way of making me realize the fact was to knock it down."

—C.S Lewis, *A Grief Observed*

"Yet one of the most essential conditions for God's grace to act in our lives is saying yes to what we are and to the situations in which we find ourselves."

—Jacques Philippe, *Interior Freedom*

FIVE

It's a Process

Will I Ever Embrace It?

I have been fortunate to spend several hours on a therapist's couch. In a small room with someone I trust with my most vulnerable self, I have processed some difficult pain points. There, my Christian counselor taught me to ask for God's insight and get curious about what He was teaching me. Mostly, I learned that healing and growth are a process.

Process is defined as "a series of actions that are needed in order to do something or achieve a result." Those steps can be painful and uncomfortable when you're working through emotional trauma. Although going through the healing process can result in clarity, hope, and a new understanding of myself, I often resist. Why? Is it because of the time required to go through it all? Is it just too uncomfortable to sit in that place of limbo, or do I just want instant results? Whichever it might be, I fight the process as much as I fight the pain.

I recently attended a gathering where one of the speakers reminded the audience of this fundamental literary truth: Every story contains a conflict. He repeated this several times for emphasis. "No conflict, no story. Let me repeat: no conflict, no story." As I heard him say it over and over, I began to feel it in my heart. My story requires conflict, and like every hero, I have the opportunity to decide how I will respond. In essence, I can write the ending to each chapter.

Don't get me wrong, I had already read about rewriting my story in the many self-help books that sit on my nightstand, but something at this moment was different. I suddenly understood the important connection between going through the process and creating a positive outcome, and that felt big. It profoundly struck me: process is key to outcome. No process, no positive outcome. Let me repeat: no process, no positive outcome. I think I always knew this deep down (and even said it to others out loud), but as I sat listening to the speaker, I was actually embracing it. I wanted to jump for joy and proclaim: "No process, no positive outcome."

Even more important, I was acknowledging that real growth happens in the process. I wish I had known about this processing pixie dust when I was younger. Instead of facing a trial or a hurt, I often ran to the busyness of life, forgoing an opportunity to grow. Yes, I was able to learn about my strength, perseverance, and that things always get better, but without processing my pain, I gained no insight or wisdom. I think I secretly feared facing it all and had no idea how God could use my suffering to grow me.

When Nono passed away (and other life trials hit), I couldn't escape the process. My grief tackled me to the ground and left me defenseless. Not even the world could draw me away from facing my despair. Furthermore, my faith had been shaken, and I couldn't hide from the fear that it caused. So, there I was on a therapist's couch, getting real about my grief and my God. I really fought it in the beginning. I remember telling my therapist I wanted to be "happy" again. I was acting a bit like a child who just wanted to take her ball and go home. I didn't want to go deeper; I wanted to feel better. I am so thankful she didn't usher me out of her office when I spoke those words. Instead, she encouraged me to walk through the pain and the process.

Sometimes I was verbally processing, and other times I was sitting in the suck (a term used by my therapist for being okay with not being okay). Feeling uncomfortable was the hardest thing for me to do, and it took everything I had to stay still without rushing to distraction. For me, it was akin to being stuck in a wet bathing suit with no towel in sight. It took patience, time, and even tears.

Thankfully, my therapist and, more importantly, God, waited for me. As I look back on the process, I believe in God's truth: He, "who called you to his eternal glory in Christ, after you have suffered a little while, will himself restore you and make you strong, firm and steadfast" (1 Peter 5:10). Processing allowed me to gain strength from my grief and deepen my faith. I now embrace it. No process, no positive outcome. Amazingly, I no longer want to be happy. I want to be complete.

I invite you to "sit in the suck" in your season of trials. Trust it's okay not to be okay and know you can process and grow. You have already done it. Don't forget that. You have seen seasons come and go, and you have persevered through

I fight the process
as much as I
fight the pain.

I didn't want to
go deeper; I wanted
to feel better.

the storms. Remember: no conflict, no story. No process, no positive outcome. You are the hero. Trust the process, and dare I say even embrace it.

> *Thank You, God, for the process as I know it can provide me with strength and deepen my faith in You.*

"The process isn't a cruel way to keep you from the promise: it's the exact preparation you'll need to handle the promise."

—Lysa Terkeurst, *It's Not Supposed To Be This Way*

"You feel what you feel and your feelings are real."

—Olaf, *Frozen 2*

"Suffering should be remedied whenever possible, but it is part of life, and attempting to get rid of it completely means suppressing life, refusing to live, and ultimately rejecting the beauty and goodness that life can bring you."

—Jacques Philippe, *Interior Freedom*

ADHD

A Dedication to Hyper-Discernment

The technical term (used today) for my over-exuberant third-grade self is Attention Deficit Hyperactivity Disorder (ADHD). Mrs. Smith (name changed to protect privacy…or I actually can't remember her name), my third-grade teacher, believed my behavior was consistent with this disorder and was happy to deliver the news to my unsuspecting parents. She encouraged them to seek not only a medical diagnosis but treatment as well. I'm sure she hoped they would look into it sooner rather than later. I mean, therapy for my ADHD would undoubtedly make her job of teaching and controlling a bunch of eight-year-olds infinitely more manageable.

As she brought her proposed diagnosis to my parents, she did not realize that their allegiance was to me, not her. My well-being, my heart, and my future were the most critical concerns for my parents, and they were not buying her "diagnosis." My dad suggested she take back her classroom and start doing her job as a teacher. He had no intention of seeking treatment for his daughter's friendly, busybody self.

My parents were confident I would soon settle down and do the necessary tasks when I realized it mattered. For the time being, I was just "overly-social." Greeting all the students as they entered the classroom and visiting with them throughout the day were in my DNA. No doubt, my parents encouraged me to follow classroom rules and the teacher's instructions (they were people of character), but they sensed no urgency to rush in and change God's design for me. They certainly had no intention of doing it through medication. Had I eventually not fallen into line, I am convinced they would have stepped in to help. But initially, they chose to wait.

I am not suggesting some kids don't struggle with ADHD and might benefit from medication. Interestingly, however, all these years later, my parent's wisdom was confirmed when I read Leonard Sax's *The Collapse of Parenting*. In his book, Sax urges parents to carefully consider the cause behind their overactive child and warns against rushing to medication as the solution. My parents' intuition was precise. Despite the urging of others, they listened within. No doubt, it would have been easier to follow the teacher's advice and help me calm down with a pill. But they walked with confidence as they determined the direction for me. How lucky am I?

This simple story about a frazzled teacher and a busy little girl highlights the way my parents lived life—trusting their decisions and walking with assurance. Free from worry, they were filled with joy. How did they do it? They believed the source of their inner voice: the Holy Spirit. They allowed Him access to each action in their lives (some seemingly small and some life or death). It's not something I can adequately explain, but it is a gift I most definitely witnessed. It's as if the veil between them and the Spirit was transparent. Their lifelong ability to tap into His voice gave them A Dedication to Hyper-Discernment (ADHD) that amazed me. I watched them live with such peace and confidence amid much uncertainty and adversity. The Holy Spirit was their Intercessor as they listened, trusted, and followed, and this was clearly evident when they chose no action with me. No pressure, no shame, only trust.

If you're wondering what happened to the classroom disruptor, I am happy to report I eventually settled down and actually excelled in school. When I figured out I could sit still, keep my mouth closed, and perform at the top of the class, I enjoyed the work. My parents were right on the mark. I eventually realized school was necessary, and I dug in with enthusiasm. I don't share this story to brag of turning around my wayward childhood or to boast about my classroom performance. Instead, I share it as a cautionary tale. Had my parents been distracted with life or too busy to deal with me, they may have rushed to implement the teacher's recommendation. Had they chosen to ignore their inner voice, they may have followed a different path. Their gut, not my teacher's observations, guided their decisions regarding me, and it gave me time to realize I was not only capable but competent. I am convinced it made all the difference in my confidence as I chose to do the work and was ready to accept responsibility.

It's as if the veil between them and the
Spirit was transparent. Their lifelong
ability to tap into His voice gave them
A Dedication to Hyper-Discernment
(ADHD) that amazed me.

I often search for His voice in the
big things but turn a deaf ear to His
guidance in the everyday life things.

I wish this inner voice victory for all of us, to seek, hear, and trust the Holy Spirit. I often search for His voice in the big things but turn a deaf ear to His guidance in the everyday life things. It's especially challenging to trust when those around me think differently. His voice, not the world's noise, is the one I need to hear. I want to let go of what others might think or what I may fear and hear the inner voice and act. God gave us this close intimacy with the Holy Spirit as a guide for our life. He can and will provide counsel if we listen to His voice. Don't ever doubt it or judge it. You can believe it and have faith in it. Let the Spirit provide wisdom to guide and protect you and your family. What a gift, what a blessing, what an incredible voice.

Thank You, God, for Your gift of the Holy Spirit. May I seek His voice and trust in His wisdom for I know it comes from You.

"Cause when you're older, absolutely everything makes sense."

—Olaf, *Frozen 2*

"I can't stop Andy from growing up... But I wouldn't miss it for the world!

—Woody, *Toy Story 2*

"I believe in you, more than anyone or anything."

—Anna, *Frozen 2*

SEVEN

My Doubting Faith and the Fear it Caused

Just One More Beautiful Puzzle Piece

Someone said life is like a puzzle, and only God understands the importance of each puzzle piece we are holding. He alone knows what the finished picture looks like. I find great comfort in this analogy and even more in realizing God knows and sees what I cannot. There have been times in my life, however, when it was challenging to stay focused on this truth.

That was the case after my mom passed away. My girls were facing trials, and my marriage was in collapse. Three separate hurts were colliding at the same time. I wasn't disappointed in God or even angry at Him over my circumstances, but I had become painfully aware of the importance of heaven and earth and a God who cared. I was hyper-focused on my faith. Instead of feeling it in my heart, I was testing it in my head. My faith was the only thing that could save me, but was it real? Could any of my essential understandings about God and heaven be true? I was reminded of these chilling words from C.S. Lewis in *A Grief Observed,* "You never know how much you really believe anything until its truth or falsehood becomes a matter of life and death to you." I was terrified. I had begun to doubt.

It's as if Satan found his "in"—my mind. He knew if he could keep God out of my heart and locked in my head, I would be filled with confusion. It was working. I was processing heaven and eternal life through my worldly view of the universe without checking the state of my heart or soul. All the trials I faced were not nearly as bad as the fear I felt as I doubted my faith. I mean, with some faith, I could handle the trials of my life, but without it, I would never survive. What was I to do with this "shaken faith" puzzle piece? It felt like I was trying to make it fit into the wrong picture. This was not part of my puzzle, and oh, by the way, neither were the hurts hurled upon me.

I have heard that questioning your faith can be an opportunity for spiritual growth. Let me tell you, when you're afraid you're losing your faith, all you want is to find your faith. My personal growth was of no concern. I was scared as I began to question everything. I desperately wanted to embrace all the things I had proclaimed before about the golden streets of heaven and the joy of being reunited with loved ones. It all felt so foreign to me now. Had I ever given real thought to the importance and consequences of those words? How would I be able to reconnect to my God—who had carried me so many times before—if I questioned His existence?

It took some outstanding Christian counseling and a very long year for me to see how God would use my doubting faith to grow me. With some serious soul searching, I began to understand how my "shaken faith" puzzle piece was actually a cry for me to build a deeper, more authentic relationship with God—a relationship based on dialogue, not Christian platitudes. I found a way to understand His existence with the aid of my heart. Slowly, I looked for God in the world around me, and I saw Him everywhere. His hand was in it all. As my heart opened to sensing His presence, I witnessed His protection and provision over me. He was there even as I questioned my connection to Him. I long to adequately describe the comfort and gentleness He provided as He paved the path back to Him. I began to understand how the "shaken faith" puzzle piece was helping me complete my final, beautiful picture (which I am still putting together).

My Christian counselor offered an analogy that perfectly describes my journey. You can observe breathtaking fish when you snorkel, but if you want to see the true majesty of the ocean, you have to scuba dive. You will have to travel through the darkest part of the water. It will be utterly black before you encounter its most exceptional beauty. My doubting faith was a call for me to scuba dive into a deeper, more beautiful relationship with God. I had to suffer through some dark interior waters, but it was worth it.

I now know (and actually feel) God's love and presence. I'm not sure I can describe the change in my heart, but I am confident it came when I released God from my head. It sounds so simple, but the terrain I walked was treacherous. I had to remember how to feel my faith, not rationalize its

All the trials I faced were not nearly as bad as the fear I felt as I doubted my faith.

Slowly, I looked for God in the world around me, and I saw Him everywhere. His hand was in it all.

existence. One of the most precious blessings was to accept my humanness and realize God's presence is not reliant on my current state of faith or belief. He waits and walks with me. That provides so much peace.

I know Satan will be waiting for me to let my faith find its way from my heart to my head. That doesn't scare me anymore. I now see a path that can lead me from fear to faith. It might be uncomfortable, but if I listen to the call to go deeper, I may find a more trusting, peaceful place.

Losing your faith might not be something you face. Whatever season of fear you find yourself in, know God will be waiting for you. He wants to show you a path and provide you with peace. It can take time, but remember, it is all part of the process. Don't worry. With God's help, you will be able to find a place for the puzzle piece you are holding that completes the picture in a way you never imagined possible.

Now go work on your puzzle, and don't fear the piece you are holding. It's all part of your beautiful life.

Thank You, God, for calling me to deeper waters where I found a more authentic relationship with You. May I always remember to encounter You first in my heart.

"You never know how much you really believe anything until its truth or falsehood becomes a matter of life and death to you. It is easy to say you believe a rope to be strong and sound as long as you are merely using it to cord a box. But suppose you had to hang by that rope over a precipice. Wouldn't you then first discover how much you really trusted it?"

—C.S. Lewis, *A Grief Observed*

"Fear can't be trusted."

—Elsa, *Frozen 2*

"By accepting the sufferings 'offered' by life and allowed by God for our progress and purification, we spare ourselves much harder ones. We need to develop this kind of realism and, once and for all, stop dreaming of a life without suffering or conflict. That is the life of heaven, not earth."

—Jacques Philippe, *Interior Freedom*

EIGHT

A Perfect Puppy in Seven Days

How a Puppy in Training Helped Me to Trust God's Plan for This Season of My Life

Oliver Beauvoir Blue Arrow was finally coming home to reside at the Mosko residence. He was eleven weeks old and could already sit, shake his paw, and lay down. I was so excited and hopeful about how easily our cute little fluff ball would transform into the obedient and regal poodle he was bred to be. We had the book (*Perfect Puppy in Seven Days*), we joined the elite dog class, and we owned one of the most intelligent canine breeds. How hard could it be?

Well, intelligent or not, this puppy had to listen to my instruction and trust my direction. We practiced and repeated the commands faithfully. We were told to complete three successful repetitions of a command before moving to the next level. Oliver was smart and quickly picked up new skills. The challenge came when distractions showed up. Shaking his paw or walking correctly on a leash became level 10 tricks when butterflies flew overhead, or, God forbid, a rabbit hopped by. Skills he had mastered suddenly became commands he had never heard when we entered new terrain. I pressed on. In the crate, out of the crate, sit, stay, shake, and rollover. Over and over.

Now as much as I love my sweet, intelligent (go with it) canine, this story is not about him becoming the perfect puppy in seven days. It's about how God used this loving crea-ture to teach me something about Himself. While I practiced the commands with Oliver, I sensed God was training and refining me. I was in a season of life where I was searching for my place. I wanted to work for God, but the path was unclear. The analogy I draw looks something like this: While I was ready to stand and fight for justice, God was telling me to sit. Although I felt a need to run and do something, God was asking me to stay. He needed my attention. When I realized the Lord was training me to focus on Him and not on my doing, I felt the weight of finding direction subside. My place was with God. Nothing else would matter if I didn't seek Him first. God was teaching me to trust His path for this season of life through the very mundane training of sitting and waiting.

It goes against my DNA to sit and wait. I think I have had a plan in place for each new day since I started kindergarten. It is now clear to me why these necessary skills are not only the most crucial instruction for my pooch but for me as well. Peace comes from knowing One greater than ourselves is in charge. Simply put, Oliver does not need to worry about his next move because he has me to direct him. I have God. What better assurance and guidance do I need? Verses I've known for some time came to mind in this new season: 'Be still, and know that I am God' (Psalms 46:10). 'My grace is sufficient for you, for my power is made perfect in weakness' (2 Corinthians 12:9). These verses now hold new meaning with the progress of my training.

I must confess, however, I am not the student Oliver has proven to be, and I find myself needing to achieve something instead of just resting in God's love. Learning to sit in complete reliance while staying focused on God is one of the hardest things I have ever done. It has, however, helped me to start trusting that I am loved and to let go of what is next. Nothing else is required. I think God has been trying to train me in this teaching my entire life: He loves me because He created me.

This is not to say God doesn't want me to do something to further the kingdom of heaven. He does. I also believe we must sometimes step out in faith before our path is clear. We walk, knowing God will provide. This, unfortunately, was not that time for me. It became clear that God was asking me to wait. I needed to believe I was created for love alone. It would be critical to any task God would ask of me, and it was proving to be the most challenging concept for me to grasp. Wait, don't go. Be patient in your nothingness. Life's activities were offering no distraction to this training, so I pressed on. In the crate, out of the crate, sit, and stay, over and over.

Oliver is almost six months old. He has already passed (with excellence) his first obedience class and is signed up to test for the Canine Good Citizen's certificate. I have no doubt

*I think God has
been trying to train
me in this teaching
my entire life: He
loves me because
He created me.*

he will advance to the next level of training as he continues the legacy of the beautiful, smart breed he represents. I hope I can do the same. I most definitely hold a deeper and more profound concept of waiting on God. With my training, I find it easier to latch onto this truth when I feel the need for accomplishment. I pray I will continue to grow in the truth of my creation, and I will look to God's Word for encouragement when I falter. "Being confident of this, that he who began a good work in you will carry it on to completion until the day of Christ Jesus" (Philippians 1:6).

I share this story in part because I want you to find great comfort in knowing the most powerful and loving force in this world loves you as you are, not for what you are doing. Let that seep deep into every fiber of your soul.

I also want you to remember that God is for you. "What, then, shall we say in response to these things? If God is for us, who can be against us?" (Romans 8:31). I am finding a deeper trust in this verse. It has taken some excellent instruction from God and lots of sit/stay repetitions from me, but I am beginning to sense the fruit of this training: a greater peace around this season of my life.

Finally, I want you to be aware of God's creativity in connecting with us. Don't be surprised when He chooses the most unlikely way to bind you with His truth. Who knew a puppy in training would help me to trust God's plan for this season of my life? May you trust all your seasons to Him and know He created you to love you.

> *Thank You, God, for creating me to love.*
> *May I rest in Your peace without the need of*
> *distractions from this world.*

"Some people talk to animals. Not many listen though. That's the problem."

—Winnie the Pooh

"First of all, the most important thing in our lives is not so much what we can do as leaving room for what God can do. The great secret of all spiritual fruitfulness and growth is learning to let God act."

—Jacques Philippe, *Interior Freedom*

"In the whole history of the world there is but one thing that money cannot buy...to wit the wag of a dog's tail."

—Josh Billings, opening line of *Lady and the Tramp*

NINE

The Fruits of His Life Were Character and Grace

The Father I Adored

My father, who left this earth far too early, was a man before his time. He possessed a lot of different qualities in the best possible combination. He was strong yet sweet-tempered, convicted yet compassionate, and confident yet caring. He championed the idea that a woman can do everything a man can and should be paid equally for it. He believed in God, loved my mom, and gave me the courage to dream for anything I wanted. He was a rock and a maverick.

How did this simple man from a small town in New Mexico with no formal education manage to climb the corporate ladder, be devoted to his family, and live a life of honor?

Character. He believed in God's path to goodness, and he followed it with conviction. You see, if you trust God's Word, you will follow His ways. It's that simple. By following God's design for his life, my dad had what a lot of people chase—faith, family, and success. He led an authentic life before it was even a thing—#dadtheoriginal.

There are so many ways he exceeded the expectation of fatherhood. He worked tirelessly to provide for our family by climbing the corporate ladder against all odds. His company knew he was special and sent him to manage-ment and computer coding school. He was one of their best programmers and recognized as one of only twelve people in the entire country who understood the programming for a specialized computer language. He believed in the people he managed, and they loved him for it. His outstanding work ethic and his fair treatment of people made him a natural leader. It's no wonder he found success in the corporate world. His kind of character is desired in all realms.

Despite all his dedication to the corporate climb, his family came first. I knew he would be at all my high school sporting events, all my dance recitals, and all the things that were important to me. He never failed, and he was always present. Now don't get me wrong. We could tangle, the two of us. I don't know if it's because we were a lot alike or because we trusted one another, but we had our differences, and we were all too happy to voice them. I could disagree with him on anything and everything, and I knew it wouldn't change his love for me. He loved me for who I was, not what I believed. That kind of love gives you the confidence to believe and trust in yourself. It provides you the courage to appreciate others without feeling the need to compare. I wish he could have lived forever, or at least long enough to meet my girls. It would have been a mutual fan club for sure.

Dad had a grace unlike anyone I have ever met. If I could live with the decency he demonstrated in his last dying months, I would consider myself a saint. He had a quiet, genuine faith and trusted God in a way that allowed him to be present with those he loved. Many have said the real test of one's character is how someone responds to adversity. His answer to pain, uncertainty, and failing health was gentleness and love. He was as kind and fun to be around in his last dying months as he had been my entire life. There was a sweetness in his eyes that made me feel loved and safe. God granted this gentle human with grace, and I was blessed to call him my dad.

He lived by following the laws and guidelines set out by His Lord and Savior. "Keep it simple," was Dad's motto. "Do the right thing now and avoid heartache later." "Put in a little extra effort, and the fruits of your labor will be abundant." "Just do the next right thing because it's always the right thing." He knew following these godly teachings would give him peace and a life he could be proud of. He was fully dedicated to that endeavor.

I have not always lived my life with such ease. I have occasionally taken what seemed an easier path at the time to find myself in an undesirable situation later. No doubt, it requires effort to do the right thing, but the reward is worth it. You might even save yourself heartache.

When my father died, I felt like my safety net had been snatched out from underneath me, and I was left uncertain.

*If I could live with
the decency he
demonstrated in his
last dying months,
I would consider
myself a saint.*

It was so hard for me to say goodbye to his peaceful soul. A lot of my confidence and assurance in this life came from his unconditional love and belief in me. He had always been the giant standing behind me as I walked the path before me. Now there was no one to back me or stand ready to shore me up. Would his training with me for this life remain when he was gone? I am blessed to report his kind of love and assurance are timeless and have stayed with my soul always.

Follow his example and keep it simple. Life may seem complicated sometimes, but if you do the next right thing, you will find these choices to be worth it. Let God's teachings guide your character, and like my father, you will be granted peace and the fulfillment we all desire.

As I said goodbye to my dad, my heart ached. I continue to long for his hug even today. I pray I have developed a character that would make him proud. I want to be a testament that God's path provides freedom and fulfillment. I also hope you find the courage to be all God has for you. I want you to know you are enough. May God's love provide you with an everlasting safety net like the one my father provided for me.

Thank You, God, for my sweet earthly father.
His character and desire to follow Your
teachings were a gift to me that I will always
cherish.

"You live what you believe, keeping conflict at a minimum.
You practice what you know, providing strength for others.
You know how to listen, giving an audience for friends.
I like it when others love you: I would not keep you for myself."
—Nancy Roberts,
"An Anniversary Letter to Ozel," *Christmas Quilt*

"Let us not become weary in doing good, for at the proper time we will reap a harvest if we do not give up."

—Galatians 6:9

"He (Ozell) understood people and situations and the universe. He knew when and how family and work and activities fit together. He didn't really struggle with life."

— Nancy Roberts, *Christmas Quilt*

TEN

Sometimes Ya Wanna Fight

How Leaning into Love and Relationship Produces the Sweetest Fruit of All

I'm typically not a fighter. Do I have lots of other vices? Yes. I can worry too much, "harp" too much, and question too much. Did I mention I do a lot of things too much? But fighting with others, especially those I love most, is not my go-to. I wish I could have held tightly to that way of thinking when a family feud erupted.

Instead, I found myself in the middle of the fight holding on to what I thought was righteous and what I thought was truth. But here is the actual truth: There is no truth when people who love each other are at odds. It's easy to hold your ground with no urgency to humble yourself when you assume everyone will live forever. It even feels good to sit tall on your self-righteous horse made of fluff. It's as if there is something noble about standing your ground on the critical issue you're defending. Never mind you are not even sure you can name the "critical issue." In fact, you fuel your own story, as you go over in your head how the events occurred and how you have been wronged. You conveniently forget the part you played and the pride you hold onto as you bolster yourself in your holier-than-thou house of cards.

But after the tragic fall and death of my beloved mother, I was faced with a choice: I could either hold tightly to the fight or embrace the humility the death of a loved one inspires. For me, it never felt like a decision. When I saw my dear family at the viewing of our mother, all my pride and self-righteousness fell away. The gift of their love and family bond overtook me. Nothing felt more right than to embrace them and share in the great grief of losing our matriarch. This was the woman who had shown us unconditional love, and the same one we had hurt over a disagreement and subsequent standoff.

I know God was waiting for our response. I also know He was confident that her tragic death would be the answer to her prayer for a family reunited. I know. I don't always sense God's providence in the moment, and I don't often know His will. But this time, I knew. It was pressed so profoundly in my soul that I have not questioned it once—and I question almost everything. It is an immense blessing when you feel God's hand in the moment. It allows you to walk with confidence and peace.

*It is an immense blessing
when you feel God's
hand in the moment. It
allows you to walk with
confidence and peace.*

*In the end, you will
benefit significantly
from the swords you
put down for love.*

I am forever grateful for the graces God provided in the family reuniting. I am also extremely aware of the lost opportunity for family connection and the deep pain the division caused my mom. That can't be changed now and looking back with regret will serve no one. But it is essential to remember how pride and self-righteousness will hurt only you and may cause you to miss out on some of life's sweetest moments.

In the end, you will benefit significantly from the swords you put down for love. Carefully consider the words you choose to hold onto as they may forever etch your heart with bitterness and ache.

Let down your armor and embrace all the happiness God holds for you in communion with the ones you love. Leaning into love and connection will always be the antidote to pride and self-righteousness. Lean in because love and relationship produce the sweetest fruit of all.

> *Thank You, God, for a family reunited and the love it has provided. May I never forget the importance of setting pride aside and the abundance connection provides.*

Nono's Wisdom: Next to Romans 1:1 she wrote this question: "Why are we so harsh on people who sin differently than we do?" She also wrote next to Romans 1:2: "Judging others is spiritually damaging. Remember what we have is a gift."

—Nono

"If you judge people, you have no time to love them."

—Mother Teresa

"You know, in spite of the fact that Christianity speaks of the cross, re-demption, and sin, we're unwilling to admit failure in our own lives. Why? Partly because it's human nature's defense mechanism against its own inadequacies. But even more so, it's because of the successful image our culture demands of us."

—Brennan Manning, *The Ragamuffin Gospel*

ELEVEN

Wiggle the Wire

On the Importance of Fond Memories and Connection with Ourselves and Others

Having a sleepover with my best friend Kelly was one of my favorite things to do growing up. I knew with certainty we would be at her house or my house every Friday night in sleeping bags on the floor. I'm not sure why we preferred this to restful sleep in our own beds, but it was a sacred tradition.

Together, we could torment anyone, and by that, I mostly mean Kelly's older sister. I'm sure she was thrilled and thankful when the sleepover was to take place at my house. Those weekends would offer her relief from two pests who became one solid force of evil when together. There wasn't anyone to torture at my house, but we could always find trouble. Many times, that meant combining our power against the boys on my block to let them know in no uncertain terms we were the Alphas. Kelly and I were champions of women long before we were even women.

Because my brother was so much older (and often out with his friends), we had the run of things at my house. Yes, my mom and dad were always there, but they never caused us any problems, and we could always rely on them for tasty snacks. They were even easy on us when it came to bedtime. While they encouraged us to close our eyes at a reasonable hour, they never nagged or complained when we greeted midnight or beyond.

Who knew the tables would turn on us one innocent weekend at my house? We were enjoying one of those nights when talking and laughing would carry us into the early morning hours. Late night Fridays were no problem for us because Saturdays were for sleeping in. You can imagine our alarm and annoyance when we were wakened by two shouting parents before the clock struck 7:00 a.m. My dad was in the attic above us shouting, "Wiggle the wire" to my mom in the basement, screeching, "What did you say?" She was much too far away to understand my dad's instruction, so they continued to shout back and forth at each other to no avail. Apparently, the early morning hours were the best time to fix a looming issue with the television. The shouting back and forth went on for several dreadful minutes until Kelly and I had both heard enough. In unison, we sat up from our slumber and cried, "Wiggle the wire!" We had simultaneously concluded our younger voices could finally relay the message and the madness could end. Two silly girls went from righteous irritation to unstoppable laughter at our impeccable timing. We were thinking the same thing at the exact time and reacted together as one. It's a memory of complete fondness I have carried with me always.

While I could stop the story at the facts, I'm compelled to dive deeper. I want to find God's greater lesson in this fun little adventure. First and most apparent is the importance of a fond memory. Did God design us to hold these precious moments so they could carry us later, if only for a minute? Did He allow us these memory lane walks to give us hope for today? I don't know about you, but when I think of a pleasant thought or joyful memory, I feel a positive physical reaction. I can actually sense both delight and peace throughout my body. I find I'm smiling at a memory I'm only playing in my head. This is a gift from God and a design only He could provide.

The story's significance I am drawn to, however, comes from the words my dad shouted to my mom—"Wiggle the wire." It's universally known we must wiggle the wire when a connection is lost. It is the first step we take to reestablish a connection. I often wiggle the wire with my fingers crossed. Who has time for a lost connection? I want to get back to my business as quickly as possible. Of course, that's rarely the case and the lost connection usually requires an in-depth analysis, tons of time, and lots of frustration before things get working again. Wiggling the wire rarely delivers. Isn't this true in life as well?

When I am out of sorts or a relationship is off, I want to find a simple solution. While I desire a quick fix, it usually requires a deeper dive. It's a plunge to understand my emotions and the part I am playing in the problem. I have

When I recognize my
wire is disconnected,
and it is a signal from
God, I feel more willing
to investigate. I have
such power over my
emotions when I invite
God to reveal and reflect
the meaning.

to admit, in previous years my lost connection included a judgment of me by me. I found myself questioning my feelings and even feeling shame. For some reason, it felt sinful to have a negative emotion. I mean, I am a woman of God and thus peachy positive is all I should feel, right?

My spiritual director helped change my perspective on emotions. She illuminated for me God's wisdom in His design for our feelings. She reminded me that feelings are neither good nor bad, but gifts from above. They indicate when something is amiss and needs attention. How comforting. When I recognize my wire is disconnected, and it is a signal from God, I feel more willing to investigate. I have such power over my emotions when I invite God to reveal and reflect the meaning. When I press toward this goal, I find reconnection more peacefully. It's not always easy, but it's always best.

I am thankful for the warning light God provides us. I wish I would have understood this when I was younger. I could have avoided a lot of wasted time wiggling the wire. I might even have denied the enemy a win over my feelings. Satan scores when he can twist our understanding of something God has actually designed for our good as something Satan created for evil. In other words, he had me convinced my negative emotions were from him and thus something to keep from God. In reality, all emotions are from God and best understood when taken to Him. What a blessing to serve a God who desires to know where we are emotionally and to help us process it completely. A God who wired us for connection and is the source of all reconnections.

A fun little story about two ornery girls will always make me smile and most definitely provide me joy. Make your

What a blessing to
serve a God who
desires to know
where we are
emotionally and
to help us process
it completely.

memories and store them carefully. God has designed us with the capability of playing them on demand and gaining real pleasure. Embrace your feelings and take them to God. Don't doubt or judge them but acknowledge and investigate them. They can provide you with a reconnection God desires for us all. I will always wiggle the wire when my computer is acting up (and laugh at my childhood memory), but I hope to seek more profound and lasting results when it comes to my emotions. How awesome to worship a God whose intricacy in our design can only bring us good.

> *Thank you, God, for the gift of our emotions.*
> *Help me to acknowledge what I am feeling so*
> *I might find the kind of connection You desire*
> *for me.*

"On any given day, she's your sister, therapist, confidante, mother, nurse, chauffeur, hair technician, clothing stylist, nutritionists, and self-help guru who proclaims that you are good enough, kind enough, and doggone it, people like you. Otherwise known as declaring, "Nobody's cuter than you!"

—Melani Shankle, *Nobody's Cuter Thank You*

"May the bonds that you build be so strong that no event or person can ever destroy, or even weaken them."

—Nancy Roberts' inscription in *Mothers and Daughters* by Lauren Cowen and Jayne Wexler

"Our girlfriends weave a luminous thread from the women we are to the women we hope to become. We many never find perfection, but we'll never be alone."

—Melani Shankle, *Nobody's Cuter Thank You*

TWELVE

Learning to Hear the Voice of God

How a Call to Act Was an Invitation to Remember God

It's no secret I am a Mother Angelica fan. Her legacy has been one of the most significant sources of encouragement and inspiration to me, especially as I navigate my second half of life. She was born Rita Rizzo and grew up in New York City. Raised by a single mother who struggled with mental issues, Rita did not have a charmed childhood and was not brought up in a stable Christian home. She faced lots of turbulence and uncertainty as a child. Nonetheless, God called her to be one of the most prominent evangelists of the modern-day Catholic Church. Through a few profound events, Mother Angelica learned about a God she could trust and a Savior she wanted to dedicate her life to.

One of my favorite Angelica traits comes from her ability to keep things simple and let God do the heavy lifting. That's how she built EWTN (Eternal Word Television Network) as a cloistered nun. It is the largest religious media network in the world, and she founded it at the ripe young age of 61. Mother Angelica knew nothing about building a cable network. Instead, she relied on her Lord as she walked through the doors He opened for her. It was that simple. Listen to God, walk through open doors, repeat. She also founded Our Lady of the Angels Monastery in Alabama, and ultimately took on the American bishops when she felt they deviated from traditional Catholic teachings. Can you imagine calling out all of the bishops? That's either real bravery or genuine trust to go where God calls.

Mother Angelica didn't have the experience, specialized knowledge, or insight into the things God was asking her to do. She trusted God would provide, and she went where He called. Angelica's spiritual teachings often instructed others to do the same. When the Holy Spirit places something on your heart, you go. Don't ask how and don't ask why; just move. God doesn't expect you to understand what you are doing, only to hear Him and to walk.

I experienced that when we started our ministry, Culture 5:11. I had no idea where it would lead when God called me to expose evils in the culture, but I knew He was asking me to walk. I am not comparing my feats to those of Mother Angelica, but I did follow her example as I moved to where God was calling. I knew I had to expose the evils of social media and pornography, but I had no experience. I had never developed a website, worked on media presentations, or presented to parents. While this might not seem like much to some, it was a lot for me. But here is the thing. My passion for exposing the culture (which God placed on my heart) drove me. I was unfamiliar with many of the things I needed to do for the cause. In fact, some of the items were utterly foreign to me, and yet most things came together quickly. I give God credit because, without His help, many of those necessary tasks would have driven me nuts, and some would have never been accomplished.

Before starting Culture 5:11, I had forgotten God's voice because doubt had set in. My spiritual director encouraged me to ponder God's purpose for me in Culture 5:11's mission. She posed a question that stirred something deep within me. How did I know it was God's voice? My answer: I had no hesitation in answering the call. I didn't second guess, and I had to act. I was confident God was asking something of me. His direction was loud and clear. As I spoke with such certainty about hearing God's call, it dawned on me: He wanted me to listen to Him because He desired me to remember Him. Through my action with Culture 5:11, I was regaining my confidence in His presence. There was no doubt and no fear in my mission. Could I transfer His voice and this trust to the more subtle moments of my life? Would I hear Him when there was no call to action, but instead only an invitation to feel His presence? Yes. The certainty He gave me in His call reignited my desire to listen. Once again, I dared to recognize His voice and push doubt away.

God's call to start Culture 5:11 may have been my invitation to remember and to trust His voice. I now understand how hearing God is a blessing I must cultivate. When I hear

Listen to God, walk through
open doors, repeat.

He wanted me to listen to
Him because He desired me
to remember Him.

Him, I need to record the sound deep within my heart. This will help me recognize Him even in a storm. It will allow me to hear Him over the noise of this world. His voice can't provide comfort if I don't know how to listen to it. How can it provide peace if I can't recognize it?

Culture 5:11 is small and reaches just a few people. I now know the number of people who hear its message or how big it becomes is not what matters. The critical thing about Culture 5:11 was for me to hear God's voice and act. God was teaching me something about Himself when He asked me to speak out. He wanted me to know I could listen and recognize His voice. I have no doubt God placed the mission on my heart, and it strengthened my faith to know He was asking something of me.

I am thankful for Mother Angelica's example to know God's voice and to step out in faith. It helped me take the critical step of walking without knowing. This provided the ultimate gift of hearing Him. You may not feel called to fight the culture, but it's important to practice listening to God. When you really observe Him, remember the sound and record the feeling on your heart, so the next time He speaks, you will know and trust His voice.

Listen carefully. God may be calling you to action or just inviting you to love Him. He's got it, and He's got you.

Thank You, God, for giving me the certainty of Your voice in my calling to Culture 5:11.

"I don't care if you're 5 or 105; God from all eternity chose you to be where you are, at this time in history, to change the world."

—Mother Angelica

"Today, if you hear his voice, do not harden your hearts as you did in the rebellion."

—Hebrews 3:15

"Unless you are willing to do the ridiculous God will not do the miraculous."

—Mother Angelica

THIRTEEN

It's Your Faith Walk, but Let Me Give You the Road Map

How Trusting God's Timing Can Be the Most Beautiful Blessing of All

Everything about our new marriage seemed perfect. Not even our faith difference seemed reason for concern. We both believed in God, so what was the big deal? The birth of our first baby girl would bring the answer to that question. Suddenly his-and-her faith was not working. There are a lot of things in a marriage that can cause stress, including finances, in-laws, work schedules, and, of course, sleep deprivation. But being religiously unequally yoked? Yep, it's a big one. Who knew? I was finding out the hard way.

OLD WOMEN SHOW YOUR ARMS AND SHARE YOUR STORIES

I became increasingly frustrated with my husband's unwillingness to attend my church and be a part of my faith. I think I secretly always felt his love for me would override his Jewish upbringing, and he would joyfully convert to Christianity. When that wasn't the case, I started many spirited debates (if that's what you want to call a heated discussion) about "true" religion. I was quickly learning how deeply grounded he was in the faith of his ancestors and how changing that conviction would require an act of God, not nagging from me.

There we were, fighting about faith—my faith. I was distraught. I wanted to be a happy little churchgoing (to my church) family. More importantly, I began to realize Stew didn't believe in the saving grace of Christ's blood on the cross. What would that mean for eternity? All of this made me more fearful and even more vocal about his conversion.

I spent a lot of time worrying about Stew while forgoing my own spiritual growth. I had little time to examine myself because I was so focused on changing another's heart. Satan always wins when he convinces me of my righteous worry. I always lose when I forget worry is never righteous and never from God.

I reluctantly realized my begging and prodding were not persuading Stew to change his faith, so I took it to God. But this time, instead of asking God to change my husband, I prayed He would reconstruct my heart. I asked God to help me trust Stew's faith walk to our Savior. I needed to let go of managing my husband's spiritual life.

*Satan always wins
when he convinces
me of my righteous
worry. I always lose
when I forget worry
is never righteous
and never from God.*

God provided. I was able to give up the dream of going to church with Stew. Instead, I was thanking God for my husband's support of raising our girls in the Catholic faith and for his willingness to attend their essential church events. He even prayed our prayers. What a blessing. Once he participated in a prayer service at the girls' school because I was unable to go. Who knew it would be an hour of kneeling and praying the Rosary? He graciously prayed. No doubt, that was a gift from God to me. Maybe a gift for Stew, too.

When I was finally able to stop putting God on a timeline for Stew's conversion, I found real freedom. I was no longer mulling over what I didn't have. I was free to recognize the blessings that were before me. A husband who supported me as I raised our children in the Catholic faith. A man who would pray our prayers and happily pay for Catholic education. Finally, a real trust that Stew's faith journey was in the hands of our Lord. That took so much self-imposed pressure off of me. I mean, it's a lot of responsibly to hold someone else's eternity.

But God already knew how the story would end. Stew converted to Catholicism after encountering the Holy Spirit in a dive Italian restaurant in Lawrence, Kansas, one weekend with Sophie. In that restaurant, over questionable food, Stew heard the Holy Spirit inviting him to a relationship with Christ. He and Sophie talked for hours and shared many tears during that rendezvous when God released His perfect timing for the conversion of Stew's heart.

I am so grateful Stew finally heard Christ's call. His conversion is one for the ages. Even the priest exclaimed it was an actual miracle. Now don't get me wrong. The most important point of this story is God's call to Stew, but equally relevant was God's promise to me. He provided me peace, and He bestowed me with trust as He answered my prayer to release Stew to Him.

I don't think trusting God's timing was my doing. I believe the strength and grace to do that came from God alone. He provided so much providence as He answered my prayer to change my heart and to trust Him with all of it—Stew's faith, the timing, and my willingness to let go.

I wish I could tell you I now faithfully give all my worries over to God. Instead, I realize how human I am. Even knowing that God provided so perfectly in Stew's faith, I find myself wanting to control life where I am fearful things won't turn out according to my plan. Those are the moments I need to humbly petition God to once again provide me with the strength to trust and let go. I have witnessed His plans, and I know His timing brings the sweetest blessings of all.

Next time you have trouble releasing your plan or a fear to God, ask Him for the gift of trust. Pray for a path to provide you faith in His providence. Ask Him, as you hold your hands open to heaven, to help you release all control and fear to Him. I promise it will give you freedom and peace like none other. I pray I will remember this as well. He can and He will carry us. We only need to ask.

Thank You, God, for Your perfect timing.
Help me to live joyfully knowing You will
always provide for me.

*I was no longer
mulling over what
I didn't have. I was
free to recognize
the blessings that
were before me.*

"Being confident of this, that he who began a good work in you will carry it on to completion until the day of Christ Jesus."

—Philippians 1:6

Nono's wisdom: God will not give up on us. He will continue to work in our lives (if we are willing) until our last days. Knowing God will be with us and wants us to prosper provides such hope. Nono was such an excellent example of this. She never stopped seeking God all the days of her life. Despite all her biblical knowledge she never assumed she knew it all. Instead, she looked first to God when in need. Her faith journey was a lifelong process, and it allowed her to get better with age. "No, dear brothers, I am still not all I should be, but I am bringing all my energies to bear on this one thing: Forgetting the past and looking forward to what lies ahead"

(Philippians 3:13, TLB).

"*Never put a lid on God. You can give God a thimble and ask for a quart. It won't work. Your plans, your projects, your dreams have to always be bigger than you, so God has room to operate. I want you to get good ideas, crazy ideas, extravagant ideas. Nothing is too much for the Lord to do.*"

—Mother Angelica

FOURTEEN

I Love My Husband, and I Always Have

The Marriage We Had and the Real Love We Found

As I write this story, I am looking into the past and exploring the feelings I held for my husband all those years ago when we met and began dating. It was a fairy tale courtship. We both had great jobs, with nothing but time and energy on our hands. We were just us. Stew wanted to do things big, and I was along for the ride. It was the perfect fit. We could talk for hours about nothing and laugh endlessly at the silliest sights. Sometimes we went on simple dates and other times, I felt like a princess. That's exactly how I felt the first time Stew picked me up for an outing. He arrived dressed to the nines, holding not one but two dozen roses. Wow. That was impressive. I was so enamored by his ability to make things happen. He was confident and in charge. I loved it.

It was a match made by God and for God. But it would be many years before we would discover how our marriage would be for God and understand His divine purpose for matrimony.

I am blessed to have a husband who cares deeply for his family and is able to provide. Stew is one of the smartest people I have ever met. He can figure things out and get things done. This held true when we had to fight for our marriage as the road became treacherous and our path unclear.

Our life together included a very uncertain and challenging detour. I think it could have caused us to lose sight of the road altogether and perhaps even to choose different ways, but God intended this marriage for a purpose. With our willingness to see what God had in store, we stepped into a healing lane with Him to explore restoration. We got curious about what God could do if we turned ourselves and our marriage over to Him. He did not disappoint. We are so blessed to have a God who cares so deeply for us.

He restored the marriage's frayed edges and provided us with a connection I would never have thought possible. Trusting our marriage to God and allowing Him to work in us through His process was the best decision we ever made. Any doubts I had about God evaporated with His work in our union. He demonstrated He was there, and He was in control as He placed people with just the right stories and expertise squarely on our path. His timing was inimitable.

As we found a way back to each other, we also found God at the center of our marriage. God provided comfort to both of us in our union and with other hurts we experienced. Through our time in that healing season, we were able to

*Trusting our
marriage to God
and allowing Him to
work in us through
His process was the
best decision we
ever made.*

draw closer to God and ultimately closer to one another. I believe this restoration was part of God's plan from the beginning. He knew we were not ready for the reality and the work it would take until later in our marriage. He waited patiently and then used our wedding vows as a way to heal both of us. I am so grateful for this recreated kinship. I have a husband and a partner I can share everything with and a man I trust more than anyone.

Why do I share this part of our life? Because I want you to know God loves marriage, and He can restore even the most broken union. I promise you there were times in that season when I felt lonely, scared, and utterly unsure if fighting to save us was even the right thing to do. Would walking away be more comfortable or somehow more righteous? I answer that question now with a resounding no. I want you to know it is worth the fight. God was a part of it and had a purpose for each of us in this holy union.

Although I always loved Stew, it was God who ultimately provided us with something intended for all marriages: trust, respect, care, and a belief that God was the reason for our connection. He refined our love so it would align with His intentions for marriage. There is nothing more unifying than knowing God has ordained your life together, and He is with you on the journey.

Don't ever hesitate to invite God into your marriage and to carry it when necessary. Call out to Him if you need His healing hand. He wants to provide you with the greatest of joy in this holy union He designed. I always loved Stew, and I always will.

*Thank you, God, for allowing me to experience
Your plan for deeper intimacy and love
through Your beautiful vocation of marriage.*

*There is nothing
more unifying than
knowing God has
ordained your life
together, and
He is with you
on the journey.*

"To love at all is to be vulnerable."

—C.S. Lewis

"Above all, love each other deeply, because love covers over a multitude of sins."

—1 Peter 4:8

"A happy marriage is the union of two great forgivers."

—Ruth Bell Graham

FIFTEEN

The Most Unlikely Season of Self-Doubt

How Turning to God for Validation is the Answer to Worthiness

Over the years, I have spent a lot of time advising others about their worth. I liked reminding my children that worth comes from above, and it is not something they can earn. While I fully believed my mantra, I would soon be tested on its validity in my own life. Would all that advice about worthiness help me when I faced my personal crisis, or would it make me feel like a complete fraud?

That was the question I asked myself when my girls were off to college, and my prestigious job title (mom in charge, CEO of family affairs, master scheduler, respected volunteer, etc.) was abruptly stripped away. What was I to do? Who would hear all my profound advice? Where would I devote my volunteer energy and what sporting team would benefit from my perfect attendance? When I could not answer those questions, I started to doubt my worth. All those years of telling my children their value came from God above seemed to elude me now. There I sat wondering what I could do to feel needed and thus worthy.

It was hard to face my doubts about who I was and what I meant to others. I never really questioned that before, and I didn't want to think about it now. This new phase of life did not bring the validation or completeness that earlier life stages included. In fact, it was quite the opposite. For the first time in my life, I had no plan, and no one (or so it seemed) was relying on me. That's when I had to recall my own words about worthiness and turn to God for validation.

Instead of relying on quotes from Brené Brown (who I often fiercely referenced) and other current-day influencers, I sought God through prayer and His Word. Don't get me wrong, I am a Brené Brown fan through and through, but my crisis would require me to sit with God and find a way to trust His unconditional love and my worth in Him. I was reminded of the Bible verses I learned as a child: 'Are not five sparrows sold for two pennies? Yet not one of them is forgotten by God. Indeed, the very hairs of your head are all numbered. Don't be afraid; you are worth more than many sparrows' (Luke 12:6-7). Who could feel forgotten reading a verse like that?

I thought of other verses reminding me of my worth: 'Let us make mankind in our image, in our likeness, so that they may rule over the fish in the sea and the birds in the sky, over the livestock and all the wild animals, and over all the creatures that move along the ground' (Genesis 1:26).

*I never realized
how much of my
worthiness tank
was filled by life's
circumstances and
the people who
surrounded me.*

Clearly, I am important to God. These verses held all the truth I needed, but had I given any deep thought to being created in God's image amidst all the distractions in my life? Did I ever sit with those words of worthiness and ponder what they meant for me? I don't think so. Or at least not in a way that would penetrate my soul and convict me of their truth when I needed it most.

I never realized how much of my worthiness tank was filled by life's circumstances and the people who surrounded me. I was unable to totally distinguish the source of my fuel until one of the resources (my title) was missing. God had always been a part of it, but in previous life phases, many other factors contributed. With my job title change from mom to empty nester, I quickly discovered God hadn't been the sole provider for my worth. It was time to start believing what I had been preaching. My worth comes from above and not from giving advice, endless volunteering, or attending important events. It doesn't even depend on my mood. God alone.

Could I believe it? I had made this sound so simple when I proclaimed it to others, but as I started my own worthiness journey, I realized it would be a process. As I went deeper into God's Word and sat with Him in silence, I felt my nothingness. At times it was lonely and even scary, but thankfully, God was patient as He continued to call me to the process. As I grieved some losses and searched for my purpose, I began to envision Christ sitting or kneeling next to me. That powerful visual enabled me to appreciate and understand God's care and concern more clearly. His Word gave me comfort, and I was grasping how I was created for Him to love me. What could provide me more worth than that?

*I am thankful for
my own struggle.
It has given me
an awareness and
depth of emotion I
previously lacked.*

I must admit, I previously didn't have an appreciation or deep compassion for the worthiness battle. Believing in your self-worth won't magically happen by quoting lines from Brené Brown. In fact, your worth may be easier to talk about than it is to feel. I am thankful for my own struggle. It has given me an awareness and depth of emotion I previously lacked. It has also highlighted God as my source of value and deepened my empathy for people who feel alone and less than. I pray I can always look to God in complete dependence and know He loves me as I am.

I wish I could tell you I have arrived and I never doubt myself. Instead, I still sometimes question if I am doing anything that matters. But here's the thing: God is all that matters in what I am doing. Do I feel like a fraud for instructing others on worth before I struggled with it myself? Not really. I am thankful to have known this important biblical teaching and happy I shared it with others.

I tell you this story for a couple of reasons. First, I want you to know I struggle with my own worthiness despite all my encouragement to others. I want you to remember to turn to God if you ever doubt your worth. You may not immediately be restored with knowing who you are in Him, but trust the process. God wants you to know your value in Him, and He will provide you with the truth.

Second, I want you to be prepared as you enter new phases of life. Don't be surprised if you feel differently about yourself or your place in the world with each new part of your journey. Don't rush to judgment. Let each phase bring the beauty it has to offer. Each will hold unique opportunities for you to experience God's love.

Finally, remember your worthiness is not tied to this world or your station in it. It's not reliant on what you are accomplishing or what people think of you. God is the source of it. So, embrace who you are in Him and all your worthiness in every phase of your beautiful life. Remind yourself of these words often because one day, you may need to rely on them for the truth.

Thank You, God, for loving me as I am.
May I remember always that You are the
source of my worth.

"Genuine self-acceptance is not derived from the power of positive thinking, mind games, or pop psychology. It is an act of faith in the God of grace."

—Brennan Manning

"He longed to become Real, to know what it felt like; and yet the idea of growing shabby and losing his eyes and whiskers was rather sad. He wished that he could become it without these"

—Margery Williams, *The Velveteen Rabbit*

"While the impostor draws his identity from past achievements and the adulation of others, the true self claims identity in its belovedness. We encounter God in the ordinariness of life: not in the search for spiritual highs and extraordinary, mystical experience, but in our simple presence in life."

—Brennan Manning, *Abba's Child*

SIXTEEN

But First Celebrate

How an Unplanned Anniversary Led to God's Validation of Our Union

It was the day of our 25th wedding anniversary, and yet I hadn't given it much thought. It's easy for me to down-play my (and by my, I mean my husband's and my) accom-plishments. What's the big deal? It's just another year. After experiencing a beautiful and meaningful anniversary celebra-tion, God changed my perspective. I am happy to now report I understand the magnitude of this marriage milestone and the importance of honoring it.

While our marriage has been full of many beautiful years, it has also had some tumultuous moments. Sometimes those hard times were a result of things thrown at us and sometimes things we brought on ourselves. We persevered. That alone is cause for celebration and, more importantly, thanksgiving to God.

I have no doubt God has been ever-present in this marriage, encouraging, nudging, and enabling us to find a way. Sometimes we followed His lead, and other times we wanted to find our own way. I promise the easiest route always came when we followed God's teachings. We found a more profound, authentic marriage when we allowed the Holy Spirit to intercede.

But here is the thing. Sometimes following God and waiting for His direction seems harder than plowing your own path. It can take patience and courage to build a relationship founded on God's design. His way does not always give immediate gratification, but it does provide lasting and real peace.

Now back to the celebration. While we didn't go on a cruise around the world or peruse the rich history in Europe, we did drive the short distance to the beautiful Broadmoor Hotel for a couple of days to honor 25 years. Not a lot of planning went into the trip. As we drove to Colorado Springs for the weekend, the importance of all our years together began to set in.

We ultimately enjoyed the most beautiful and celebratory anniversary I could have ever imagined. It included long walks, fabulous dinners, and lots of conversations about all our years together. Probably the most meaningful and beautiful aspect of that weekend was attending confession and then mass together as a couple. The priest even congratulated us before the congregation and joked that all the parishioners should join us for an anniversary dinner (on us) after mass. The power of including God and recognizing His providence over our marriage was the most magical

We found a more profound, authentic marriage when we allowed the Holy Spirit to intercede.

part of our weekend together. It solidified our union and its importance in the eyes of God.

No, not every year of our marriage was fabulous, but every year held purpose. Each twelve months led us to a deeper and more meaningful life together. Sometimes the hardest years brought the most growth. All mattered and all should be celebrated. Sometimes in the midst of a journey, it's impossible to see the progress, but I promise it's happening. C.S. Lewis said it best when he noted, "Isn't it funny how day by day nothing changes, but when you look back, everything is different." That's why it is so important to celebrate each year, to realize and recognize how God will use each one to grow your union. Trust He can accomplish this in your joined journey.

So, yes, celebrate. Celebrate each and every year of your marriage. Celebrate not only the milestones you pass with your spouse but all your individual accomplishments along the way. There will be plenty of ordinary times, but those special moments must be recognized.

Let God celebrate with you, too. Allow Him in those joyous times as He will carry you in the trials. This is your life! Celebrate!

Thank You, God, for celebrating with us.
May we always remember to include You in
our rejoicing, as we know it is You who will
carry us in the trials.

*His way does
not always
give immediate
gratification, but it
does provide lasting
and real peace.*

"Be completely humble and gentle; be patient, bearing with one another in love. Make every effort to keep the unity of the Spirit through the bond of peace."

—Ephesians 4:2-3

"For this is one of the miracles of love: It gives – to both, but perhaps especially to the woman - a power of seeing through its own enchantments and yet not being disenchanted."

—C.S. Lewis, *A Grief Observed*

"Some people are worth melting for."

—Olaf, Frozen 2

SEVENTEEN

Follow Your Dreams and Eat Your Peas

A Love Letter to My Grandchildren

This story (really more of a love letter) is to my precious souls who have not yet entered this world, but who undoubtedly will bring great joy to their Heavenly Father and earthly parents. I want my grandchildren to know how much I love them, and I will be praying for their path. May God fill it with abundant joy and great wisdom from Him.

I love you and I haven't even held you. My greatest desire is for you to understand you will never be alone. Walk this earth with confidence and courage because the most supreme force in all the universe loves you as you are. I think I spoke similar words to your parents, but I want you to trust this truth as well.

May you always find laughter and comfort in the simple things of life. Might you appreciate the importance of family and accept you can't have it all. Choose wisely where you give of your time and remember to guard your heart. Most importantly, live. Follow your heart and your dreams and sometimes eat your peas—but mostly follow your dreams.

With all my love, care, and heart, I will forever be petitioning protection over your life. I will always be standing with you and for you—forever.

With much love and many hugs,

Your devoted, doting YaYa

> *Thank You, God, for the gift of life. Please protect my precious grandchildren and grant them Your providence as they journey this life.*

*Walk this earth with
confidence and
courage because the
most supreme force
in all the universe
loves you as you are.*

"My love is not fragile."

—Kristoff, *Frozen 2*

"You're braver than you believe and stronger and smarter than you think."

—Winnie-the-Pooh

"When I look at you, I can feel it. I look at you, and I'm home."

—Finding Nemo

EIGHTEEN

The Gift of Wonder

May You Practice It, Share It, and Receive the Grace in It

In *The Ragamuffin Gospel*, Brennan Manning tells us a story about an older rabbi who is on his deathbed. When the rabbi's good friend pays him a visit in his last hours, he tells him that he is dying a happy man. The rabbi goes on to say that he never asked God for fame and fortune but simply requested the gift of wonder. *How beautiful*, I thought. But Manning reminds the reader that, "By and large, our world has lost its sense of wonder. We have grown up. We no longer catch our breath at the sight of a rainbow or the scent of a rose, as we once did." *How true*, I thought. Had I forgotten how to slow down and admire the natural gifts around me?

This struck me deeply. It made me question my own ability to pause and see all God's majesty before me. I realized how the gift of wonder, which once provided an outlet and even a diversion to thinking about self, doesn't get a moment's thought in our culture today. I must admit I am often not interested in or curious about the natural phenomenon or beauty around me. I am far too busy returning emails or completing the day's task to take in God's handiwork.

It dawned on me that this beautiful gift of wonder is clearly a sister to gratitude and meant to bring us comfort. When I am curious about nature and its intricacies, it is difficult for me to also consider my troubles. When I am thanking God for my blessings, it distracts me from what I am lacking. Wonder and gratitude can offer relief from self and provide hope for all we possess, both materially and spiritually.

Maybe that is why many spiritual retreats take place in nature. What better place to find God than the very landscape He created? How could you not feel His presence in all the wonder He designed? I am getting ready to embark on a spiritual retreat where I pray I will hear God's direction for my life. The mission for this retreat, however, is shifting. Instead of needing something from God, I hope I can just relax in the wonder of His making and find comfort and appreciation in a God who loves me. Can I let go of requesting and be present for receiving?

As highlighted by Brennan Manning, "God intended for us to discover His loving presence in the world around us." No doubt, St. Therese agreed when she said, "Far away on the horizon we could see the great mountains....The sight of these beauties made a deep impression on my thoughts; I felt as if I were already beginning to understand the greatness of God and the wonder of heaven." We have an awesome God who has provided us a source of greatness and comfort at no cost and with little searching. We can have a glimpse

*It dawned on me
that this beautiful
gift of wonder is
clearly a sister to
gratitude and meant
to bring us comfort.*

of heaven with a simple walk through nature or a look toward the sky. This alone should provide us with a bounty of gratitude.

I would like to feel the peace of Brennan Manning's rabbi. I pray I will seek God in His gift of wonder, and I will be ever grateful for the soul care He provides in the beauty around me. Don't forget to look around or to look up the next time you are feeling stressed. It may just be the antidote to whatever ails you and be an important reminder of God's love and care.

Thank You, God, for the gift of wonder. May I remember to look for Your love and care in all the beauty in the world around me.

*Instead of needing
something from God,
I hope I can just
relax in the wonder
of His making and
find comfort and
appreciation in a
God who loves me.*

"The heavens are yours, and yours also the earth; you founded the world and all that is in it."

—Psalm 89:11

"We get so preoccupied with ourselves, the words we speak, the plans and projects we conceive, that we become immune to the glory of creation."

—Brennan Manning, *The Ragamuffin Gospel*

"We need to find God, and he cannot be found in noise and restlessness. God is the friend of silence. See how nature — trees, flowers, grass — grows in silence; see the stars, the moon and the sun, how they move in silence... We need silence to be able to touch souls."

—Mother Teresa

NINETEEN

The Drop Off

The Emotion It Brings is the Theme of Motherhood and the Slow Transitioning of Parenthood

I had just dropped Sophie off in downtown Denver for a post-grad job interview. The cost of parking and other logistics led me to offer her my chauffeuring services. As I sat waiting in my car, drinking lukewarm coffee, I was reminded of all the childhood drop-offs on this parenting journey and my mind began to spin.

From dropping Victoria off on her first day of preschool to leaving Sophie for her freshmen year of college, I was struck by the number of times I had said goodbye and good luck as one of my daughters exited my parked car. I felt like I had been transported back in time. I could almost feel Victoria releasing her tiny hand from mine as she slowly made her way to the preschool room. As she walked toward her teacher, she looked back at me. All my pride and fear rushed in as I looked into her beautiful brown eyes. Oh, the pain in my heart. I would feel those same emotions several years later as Sophie started her college adventure in another state. Fours years would feel like a lifetime. It suddenly occurred to me how all the drop-offs and subsequent good-byes were a theme of motherhood. Many of the emotions I had felt over the years of loving and caring for my girls were somehow intensified and magnified with the drop-off. As those memories streamed in, tears streamed down my face.

How could those exciting moments for my sweet little girls be filled with tears of grief for me? Didn't I want them to grow up and become self-supporting young women? Hadn't I dreamt of that with each tuition check I wrote? The answer was yes, but the consequence a jolt. All those previous drop-offs were slowly and subtly preparing me to release my daughters back to their Heavenly Father. No doubt, they were always in His care, but the role I played slowly diminished each time I uttered "goodbye and good luck."

As the tears ran on, I sat in my car and remembered back. It felt as if all the emotions of motherhood were plummeting on me at once. I could almost feel all the highs of each daughter's triumph, and the heartbreak of her inevitable defeats. The gift of watching them grow had come with the cost of sharing in their grief—a burden I willingly accepted. I endured their sorrows so I could know their joy. The clashing of those opposing emotions felt like a boulder on my soul. It was the ultimate lesson in empathy. I could not choose it; I just felt it. Definitely more tears. I sat there and pondered what it all meant for me. What would God reveal as the highlight reel of emotions played on in my head?

The early morning clouds began to dissipate, and my mood gave way to extreme appreciation. God's lesson pierced my heart, and I realized He had given me the unique blessing of vicariously experiencing both the mountain tops and desert

The gift of watching them grow had come with the cost of sharing in their grief—a burden I willingly accepted. I endured their sorrows so I could know their joy.

valleys through the lives of my daughters. What greater honor than to walk this earth with two souls entrusted so intentionally to me? It struck me deeply. Would all the widely passionate emotions of motherhood be a prelude to the adoration I would feel for God and all His creation when I journeyed home to heaven? Was this just a glimpse of the glory yet to come? As the tears slowed, my gratitude grew.

Reality started to creep back in, and I looked at the clock, wondering how much time I had spent mesmerized by all the emotions of the drop-off. I was also curious about the feelings that would greet me as Sophie finished her interview and reentered the car. Would she be excited about all the possibilities in this potential job or worried about her path?

Whatever would come, I was ready to embrace it because my focus had shifted to gratitude. What a blessing to learn compassion through the very routine chore of the drop-off. Who knew all the emotions in "goodbye and good luck" were delicately teaching me empathy while preparing me for a new phase of parenting?

God had so wisely planned my journey. He slowly and methodically ordered my steps and prepared me for what was ahead—fewer drop-offs and the capacity for more understanding. I knew He had trained me, and I wanted to trust Him in my transition from driver to the back seat of the car. While it will hold less control, it will undoubtedly require more empathy as they find their own paths. If I let go and let God, it might just be the best ride yet.

Thank You, God, for ordering my steps on this parenting journey. May I embrace this new phase and willingly adjust my role as a parent of adult children.

*Would all the widely
passionate emotions
of motherhood be a
prelude to the adoration
I would feel for God
and all His creation
when I journeyed
home to heaven?*

"And so time went on, and the little Rabbit was very happy—so happy that he never noticed how his beautiful velveteen fur was getting shabbier and shabbier, and his tail coming unsewn, and all the pink rubbed off his nose where the Boy had kissed him."

—Margery Williams, *The Velveteen Rabbit*

"Let it go! Let it go! Can't hold it back anymore!"

—Elsa, *Frozen 2*

"Train a child in the way he should go, and when he is old he will not turn from it."

—Proverbs 22:6

TWENTY

The Last

How a World Pandemic Changed Everything and Reminded Me of Nono's Words

As I started this collection of stories, I was reminded of the words Nono wrote on the last page of her Bible. They held meaning for her and have been a source of comfort to me. And now, given the devastation and fear circling the globe, these words provide more peace than I could possibly imagine. How comforting to know that God:

Is good.

Is in control.

Can be trusted.

COVID-19 (a novel virus) arrived on the scene, causing complete confusion in early 2020. In fact, the virus has often been compared to a biblical plague. Writing this feels more like a fiction short story than a recounting of facts.

While the virus originated in China, it quickly made its way to the U.S. Symptoms, although similar to the common cold, can cause hospitalization and even death. What?! The difference between a few sneezes and death is horrific. Which would it be and for whom? With the infiltration of the virus into each state, we fear COVID 19 will kill more people than any other infection to date. More frightful yet is knowing it is highly contagious. Equally unnerving is hearing the death totals in the daily news. It all feels like something out of a horror movie.

As if all this wasn't enough, the government has ordered everyone to stay home and wear masks when out in public. Although we are allowed to go outdoors for exercise, we are encouraged to maintain a distance of at least six feet from other people. As I walk around the neighborhood, I find myself in a mode of hyper-awareness, surveying the terrain to determine my appropriate distance from fellow neighbors. I frequently have to cross the street to avoid close contact with passersby. As I greet others, I see only their eyes peering back at me because the rest of their face is covered with some sort of makeshift mask. Contrary to the lyrics in many country songs, the eyes do not tell all, and I am often left wondering about the greeting I am receiving.

I must confess all of it makes me somewhat uncomfortable. I worry I am not keeping a safe distance and am fearful things will never return to normal. While I don't want to offend anyone with my behavior, I am vigilant about following the rules. No doubt, these drastic measures are essential to save precious lives, but the precautions will undoubtedly come at a price. Lives will be disrupted, an economic recession will

*I need to recognize
where I stand
spiritually amongst
all this disarray.
Without knowing
that, how can I
grow in my faith?*

ensue, and social interactions will change forever. It seems surreal, and I wonder if all this is a part of a coma-induced dream.

In reality, nothing has served to more correctly order the world's affairs than the fear surrounding this virus. Countries are more appropriately focused on the potential loss of life than the almost certain loss of jobs. Leaders are working feverishly to devise safe and reliable ways to fight the virus, and individuals are sacrificially doing their part to keep others safe by staying home. In this unprecedented time in history, I feel enormous gratitude. It is by far my overriding emotion. Our family is well, and we all reside in the same state. We have plenty of food and are blessed to have a home. Finally, I am the ultimate homebody, and sheltering in place is no real hardship for me.

In some ways, I have been preparing for this moment my entire life. Washing my hands for at least 20 seconds and assessing surrounding surfaces for possible contaminates is nothing for me. Not touching my face—easy. Cleaning and recleaning surfaces is a daily task I gladly greet. Who knew my slightly obsessive personality would eventually come in handy and allow me to meet this new norm with such ease?

Not as easy for me is the loss of human connection. While I thoroughly enjoy my family engagement with Sophie and Stew, I have missed the face-to-face time and hugs from Victoria and her fiancé, Jarod. Unable to share Easter with my extended family or to celebrate the Risen Christ in a packed and glorious church feels heartbreaking. Further, I despise having to greet neighbors from a distance, and I hate the thought of not visiting with my friends in person. I know these feelings aren't unique to me, but acknowledging them feels so good. Nonetheless, I press on with my distancing in the effort to help flatten the curve.

As with all my stories, I want to share my experience of God in this reality. No doubt, He is watching over the unfolding events with great sadness. He wired us for connection with the ones we love. Seeing His people suffer and even succumb to death has never been a part of His plan.

If this is going to hold personal meaning, I've got to get curious about God's soul message for me in the madness. Simply put, I can't be a bystander or onlooker to the world in crisis. I have to stretch my faith and ask God specifically about the spiritual teaching for me. I must admit it is tempting to forgo the exercise. I could conveniently convince myself I am much too busy managing the problem to learn something about myself in God.

If there is one thing I have gained in this life, however, it's to know God wants to strengthen my relationship with Him through all my circumstances. Just as He called out to Adam and Eve about their whereabouts in the garden, He is questioning the same of me. I need to recognize where I stand spiritually amongst all this disarray. Without knowing that, how can I grow in my faith?

Cue a super spine-chilling contaminant from another continent to encourage my inventory of faith. Can I look inward to access the state of my heart? Can I put aside worry about COVID-19 to better myself? In *Dangerous Prayers*, the author notes, "What we fear the most often reveals where we trust God the least." Truthfully, these words are more frightful to me than the global pandemic itself. Can I handle what God will reveal and then allow Him to lead me to trust? History proves my greatest peace comes when I search inward for my needs and then upward for fulfillment. Based on God's impeccable track record, I can trust He will heal and deliver me with the most excellent comfort from all that ails me. Let Him do the same for you.

The pandemic will pass, but other fears will come. The God of all mercy is here to empathically walk with us. While we must social-distance from neighbors and others, we can always choose closeness to God. He is the consistent comforter, and His greatest desire is peace. I prefer Him over fear, and I am forever grateful for His walk with me in this epic pilgrimage called life.

Thank You, God, for Your consistent comfort in my pilgrimage of life. I sense You and love You and I am so ever grateful for Your persistent presence.

*History proves
my greatest peace
comes when I
search inward
for my needs and
then upward for
fulfillment.*

"If we go to the depths of anything, we will begin to knock upon something substantial, 'real,' and with a timeless quality to it. We will move from the starter kit of 'belief' to an actual inner knowing. This is most especially true if we have ever (1) loved deeply, (2) accompanied someone through the mystery of dying, (3) or stood in genuine life-changing awe before mystery, time, or beauty."

—Richard Rohr, *Falling Upward*

"*The most important and most fruitful acts of our freedom are not those by which we transform the outside world as those by which we change our inner attitude in light of the faith that God can bring good out of everything without exception.*"

—Jacques Philippe, *Interior Freedom*

"People who have had no inner struggles are invariably both superficial and uninteresting. We tend to endure them more than communicate with them, because they have little to communicate."

—Richard Rohr, *Falling Upward*

FINAL THOUGHTS

Looking Back and Going Forward

My Hope for You in These Stories

As I gather these stories for you, I am asking myself why I began this project in the first place. Two reasons stand out for me. First, I want my daughters to know they are not alone, and my heart and prayers will be with them even when I have passed from this life. I hope it helps them to know I am forever tethered to them, and I have boundless confidence in God's provision over their lives.

Second, I know the Holy Spirit placed this writing on my heart. I must admit, I never really considered spending focused time completing this project or getting it into a book format. That changed on June 13, 2019, when I wrote in my journal, "I have to finish stories." I remember I had been listing possibilities on where to focus my energy, and I wrote with confidence to "finish my stories." I can't explain the emotion or conviction I felt, but the Holy Spirit was encouraging me to prioritize the task, and I knew I must try.

I, too, have experienced
both the summit and the
basin and know both
are reminders of the
importance of gratitude.

It's a reminder to choose
wisely as we walk, because
life inevitably evolves.

My greatest hope is for you to find comfort in my words. This life will offer you beautiful and bountiful moments, as well as trials and tests. I, too, have experienced both the summit and the basin and know both are reminders of the importance of gratitude. Each season of life will offer an opportunity to invite God in to show you all He has for you. Let Him walk with you and your family. His path will provide the most significant source of contentment.

Although I wrote these stories primarily for my girls, they have been a source of encouragement for me. They have been a reminder of God's goodness and His protection over me, especially in my most trying times. They are a witness to me of God's desire to draw me in and proof of my calmness in Him. C.S. Lewis's words were so telling when he wrote: "Isn't it funny how day by day nothing changes, but when you look back, everything is different?" This has been heavy on my heart with the writing of these stories. It's a reminder to choose wisely as we walk, because life inevitably evolves.

I can't wait to see all the glorious seasons yet to come for both Victoria and Sophie. There is so much ahead and so many opportunities to receive God's love. May they desire God's wisdom and know they are protected. Whatever this life may hold, may they know I am keeping them in my prayers and on my heart always.

Victoria and Sophie, you are forever imprinted on my soul. —Mama

Thank You, God, for all of it. May I seek You in all my stories yet to come.

In memory of Nancy Roberts

In memory of the woman who followed her dreams, cared for our hearts, and loved her God. Nancy Roberts, your love is forever etched on our souls. Until we meet again.

"Hold fast to dreams, for if dreams die, life is a broken-winged bird that cannot fly."

—Langston Hughes

On Love

"God loves me. I'm not here just to fill a place, just to be a number. He has chosen me for a purpose. I know it."

—Mother Teresa, *The Love that Made Mother Teresa*

"When are you going to see yourself how I do?"

—Anna, *Frozen 2*

"There is no fear in love. But perfect love drives out fear, because fear has to do with punishment."

—1 John 4:18

On Grief

"For in grief nothing 'stays put.' One keeps on emerging from a phase, but it always recurs. Round and round. Everything repeats. Am I going in circles, or dare I hope I am on a spiral?

But if a spiral, am I going up or down it?

How often -- will it be for always? -- how often will the vast emptiness astonish me like a complete novelty and make me say, 'I never realized my loss till this moment'? The same leg is cut off time after time."

—C.S. Lewis, *A Grief Observed*

"No one ever told me that grief felt so like fear. I am not afraid, but the sensation is like being afraid. The same fluttering in the stomach, the same restlessness, the yawning. I keep on swallowing.

At other times it feels like being mildly drunk, or concussed. There is a sort of invisible blanket between the world and me. I find it hard to take in what anyone says. Or perhaps, hard to want to take it in. It is so uninteresting. Yet I want the others to be about me. I dread the moments when the house is empty. If only they would talk to one another and not to me."

—C.S. Lewis, *A Grief Observed*

"Part of every misery is, so to speak, the misery's shadow or reflection: the fact that you don't merely suffer but have to keep on thinking about the fact that you suffer. I not only live each endless day in grief, but live each day thinking about living each day in grief."

—C.S. Lewis, *A Grief Observed*

On Faith

"God didn't call me to be successful. God called me to be faithful."

—Mother Teresa

"Our freedom is, in fact, proportionate to the love and childlike trust we have for our heavenly Father."

—Jacques Philippe, *Interior Freedom*

"God has not been trying an experiment on my faith or love in order to find out their quality. He knew it already. It was I who didn't. In this trial He makes us occupy the dock, the witness box, and the bench all at once. He always knew that my temple was a house of cards. His only way of making me realize the fact was to knock it down."

—C.S Lewis, *A Grief Observed*

On Process

"But when we see that God's purpose is good, we can trust His process is good."

—Lysa Terkeurst, *It's Not Supposed To Be This Way*

"God is who He says He is, and He will do what He says He will do. But to partner with Him in His work of transformation in our lives, we must seek Him with all our hearts. It's our choice whether we stay stuck in our hurt or get renewed in our hearts."

—Lysa Terkeurst, *It's Not Supposed To Be This Way*

"We will not receive the grace to change unless we desire to; but to receive the grace that will transform us, we must 'receive' ourselves – to accept ourselves as we really are."

—Jacques Philippe, *Interior Freedom*

On Suffering and Healing

"God isn't far off. He's just far more interested in your being prepared than in your being comfortable."

    —Lysa Terkeurst, *It's Not Supposed To Be This Way*

"Life, as the biblical tradition makes clear, is both loss and renewal, death and resurrection, chaos and healing at the same time: life seems to be a collision of opposites."

    —Richard Rohr, *Falling Upward*

"Without your wound where would your power be?"

    —Thornton Wilder, *The Angel that Troubled the Waters*
    (restated from Brennan Manning's *Abba's Child*)

On Grace

1) "The deeper we grow in the Spirit of Jesus Christ, the poorer we become- the more we realize that everything in life is a gift."

—Brennan Manning, *The Ragamuffin Gospel*

2) Nono's wisdom: Next to Matthew 25:29 she wrote: "Time, talent, treasures: give of them." I witnessed her give of all of these throughout her lifetime. Nono gave herself to others with her time and talent, and God was faithful to His Word with the abundance He in turn gave her. "For the man who uses well what he is given shall be given more and he shall have abundance. But from the man who is unfaithful, even what little responsibility he has shall be taken from him"

—(Matthew 25:29, TLB).

"The grace of the Lord Jesus be with God's people. Amen."

—Revelation 22:21

About the Author

With a finance degree from the University of Colorado and an MBA from the University of Denver, Kim Roberts Mosko was all about her career and loved working in commercial real estate investing. With the birth of her two daughters, that all changed, and Kim followed the tug on her heart to leave the corporate world behind and start a new adventure at home with her sweet little girls.

Kim treasures the time she had with her daughters. Every day, she saw glimpses of God's heart for her through the joy of spending time with her daughters. She and her husband Stew loved spending time with their girls and spent many hours in volleyball gyms cheering them on. Now twenty-two and twenty-six, Kim's daughters are no longer in their home, but they continue to fill their hearts.

Empty-nesting and life trials caused doubts Kim had never before known. That's when God invited her to become more rooted and to trust in Him. Through that time, Kim realized He had been with her always—through every season and every story.

In *Old Women Show Your Arms and Share Your Stories*, Kim shares how she found God's persistent presence in her everyday life. She writes from her heart to her journal and now to the book you hold in your hands. She prays it will be a source of encouragement for her daughters, as well as a reminder of God's perpetual presence to lift your soul.

Stew and Kim continue to live in the home where they raised their family. It is their greatest desire to grow up with their girls and provide them with love and support that respects their adult standing. She also hopes they embrace each day with the wonder and grace reminiscent of earlier life phases. No doubt raising their new fur puppy, Oliver, will offer them that unique opportunity.

Acknowledgements

Thank you, God, for Your presence in my stories and for the promise of Psalm 23. I find perfect peace in the words of the Psalmist who wrote: "Surely goodness and love will follow me all the days of my life, and I will dwell in the house of the Lord forever." May I seek You always.

Thank you, Stew, for your ever-willing spirit. God has used our love to teach me so much about Him – is that not the very meaning of marriage? I love you.

Thank you, Victoria and Sophie, for providing me a love I cannot contain. You give me purpose and a hope that surly resemble heaven above. I am forever grateful for our closeness both in proximity and even more prominently in our hearts.

Thank you, Renee Fisher, for both challenging and encouraging me. You are such a witness to keeping God in the story. I wrote in my journal that God has placed the right people in my path. You are no exception. You make things happen.

Thank you, Rebekah Benham, for going above and beyond. Your attention to detail and your honesty provided me much needed confidence. You taught me so much.

Thank you, Nelly Murariu, for your creativity in capturing my heart and intention in the cover. Your talent is amazing and your patience and sweetness a blessing to the process.

Thank you, Melanie Chitwood, for your careful review and encouraging comments – they created more motivation then you know.

Sources

Foreword

Brennan Manning, *Ragamuffin Gospel* (Sisters, Oregon: Multnomah Press, 2005), 14.

Brennan Manning, *Ragamuffin Gospel* (Sisters, Oregon: Multnomah Press, 2005), 14.

Introduction

Mother Angelica, quoted in Shaun McAfee, "20 Brilliant, Sharp, and Witty Quotes from Mother Angelica," EpicPew, March 30, 2016, https://epicpew. com/20-brilliant-sharp-and-witty-quotes-from-mother-angelica.

One

Margery Williams Bianco and William Nicholson, *The Velveteen Rabbit, or, How Toys Become Real* (London: Doubleday Children's, 2014), 5.

Two

A.A. Milne, *Winnie-the-Pooh*, quoted in "Quotable Quote," Goodreads, accessed May 29, 2020, https://www.goodreads.com/ quotes/51437-some-people-care-too-much-i-think-it-s-called-love.

Three

A.A. Milne, *Adventures of Winnie-the-Pooh*, quoted in "Quotable Quote," Goodreads, accessed May 29, 2020, https://www.goodreads.com/ quotes/223700-what-day-is-it-asked-pooh-it-s-today-squeaked-piglet.

Jacques Philippe, *Interior Freedom* (New York: Scepter Publishers, 2007), 58.

Raymond Arroyo, *Mother Angelica: the Remarkable Story of a Nun, Her Nerve, and a Network of Miracles* (New York: Image Books, 2007), 137.

Four

Mother Angelica, "Mother Angelica Quotes and Sayings," Inspiring Quotes, accessed May 30, 2020, https://www.inspiringquotes.us/ author/1460-mother-angelica.

C.S. Lewis, *A Grief Observed* (New York: Harper One, n.d.), 52.

Jacques Philippe, *Interior Freedom* (New York: Scepter Publishers, 2007), 32.

Five

"Process," Cambridge Dictionary, accessed May 30, 2020,
https://dictionary.cambridge.org/dictionary/english/process.

Lysa TerKeurst, *It's Not Supposed to Be This Way: Finding Unexpected Strength When Disappointments Leave You Shattered* (Nashville: Thomas Nelson, 2018), 102.

Frozen 2, directed by Jennifer Lee and Chris Buck (2019; Burbank, CA: Walt Disney Animation, 2020), DVD.

Jacques Philippe, *Interior Freedom* (New York: Scepter Publishers, 2007), 48.

Six

Frozen 2, directed by Jennifer Lee and Chris Buck (2019; Burbank, CA: Walt Disney Animation, 2020), DVD.

Toy Story 2, directed by Ash Brannon, John Lasseter, and Lee Unkrich (1999; Burbank, CA: Disney/Pixar, 2001), DVD.

Frozen 2, directed by Jennifer Lee and Chris Buck (2019; Burbank, CA: Walt Disney Animation, 2020), DVD.

Seven

C.S. Lewis, *A Grief Observed* (New York: Harper One, n.d.), 22.

C.S. Lewis, *A Grief Observed* (New York: Harper One, n.d.), 22-23.

Frozen 2, directed by Jennifer Lee and Chris Buck (2019; Burbank, CA: Walt Disney Animation, 2020), DVD.

Jacques Philippe, *Interior Freedom* (New York: Scepter Publishers, 2007), 49.

Eight

A.A. Milne, *Winnie-the-Pooh*, quoted in "Quotable Quote," Goodreads, accessed May 30, 2020, https://www.goodreads.com/quotes/29556-some-people-talk-to-animals-not-many-listen-though-that-s.

Jacques Philippe, *Interior Freedom* (New York: Scepter Publishers, 2007), 32.

Josh Billings, quoted in "Quotable Quote," Goodreads, accessed May 30, 2020, https://www.goodreads.com/quotes/276622-in-the-whole-history-of-the-world-there-is-but.

Nine

Nancy Roberts, *Christmas Quilt* (self-pub., iUniverse.com, 2003), 61.

Nancy Roberts, *Christmas Quilt* (self-pub., iUniverse.com, 2003), 46.

Ten

Mother Teresa, quoted in "Quotes," Goodreads, accessed May 30, 2020, https://www.goodreads.com/author/quotes/838305.Mother_Teresa.

Brennan Manning, *Ragamuffin Gospel* (Sisters, Oregon: Multnomah Press, 2005), 175.

Eleven

Melanie Shankle, *Nobody's Cuter than You: a Memoir about the Beauty of Friendship* (Carol Stream, IL: Tyndale House Publishers, 2015), 220.

Melanie Shankle, *Nobody's Cuter than You: a Memoir about the Beauty of Friendship* (Carol Stream, IL: Tyndale House Publishers, 2015), 198.

Twelve

Mother Angelica, quoted in "Everything Starts with One Person," Inspiring Quotes, accessed May 30, 2020, https://www.inspiringquotes.us/quotes/vi5Y_27v3kyAF.

Raymond Arroyo, *Mother Angelica: the Remarkable Story of a Nun, Her Nerve, and a Network of Miracles* (New York: Image Books, 2007), 146.

Thirteen

Mother Angelica, quoted in "Mother Angelica Quotes," PrimoQuotes, accessed May 30, 2020, https://www.primoquotes.com/author/mother+angelica.

Fourteen

C.S. Lewis, *A C.S. Lewis Treasury: Three Classics in One Volume* (New York: Harcourt Brace & Co., n.d.), 121.

Ruth Graham Bell, quoted in "Quotable Quote," Goodreads, accessed May 30, 2020, https://www.goodreads.com/quotes/895079-a-happy-marriage-is-the-union-of-two-good-forgivers.

Fifteen

Brennan Manning, *Ragamuffin Gospel* (Sisters, Oregon: Multnomah Press, 2005), 49.

Margery Williams Bianco and William Nicholson, *The Velveteen Rabbit, or, How Toys Become Real* (London: Doubleday Children's, 2014), 8.

Brennan Manning, *Abba's Child* (Colorado Springs, CO: NavPress, 2015), 33-34.

Sixteen

C.S. Lewis, quoted in "A Quote by C.S. Lewis," Goodreads, accessed May 30, 2020, https://www.goodreads.com/ quotes/7601569-isn-t-it-funny-that-day-by-day-nothing-changes-but.

C.S. Lewis, *A Grief Observed* (New York: Harper One, n.d.), 72.

Frozen 2, directed by Jennifer Lee and Chris Buck (2019; Burbank, CA: Walt Disney Animation, 2020), DVD.

Seventeen

Frozen 2, directed by Jennifer Lee and Chris Buck (2019; Burbank, CA: Walt Disney Animation, 2020), DVD.

A.A. Milne, *Winnie-the-Pooh*, quoted in "Quotable Quote," Goodreads, accessed May 30, 2020, https://www.goodreads.com/quotes/7684158-you-re-braver-than-you-believe-and-stronger-and-smarter-than.

Finding Nemo, directed by Andrew Stanton and Lee Unkrich (2003; Burbank, CA: Walt Disney Animation, 2013), DVD.

Eighteen

Brennan Manning, *Ragamuffin Gospel* (Sisters, OR: Multnomah Press, 2005), 90.

Brennan Manning, *Ragamuffin Gospel* (Sisters, OR: Multnomah Press, 2005), 91.

Carmen Britos, "A Sense of Wonder: Nature and St. Therese," Society of the Little Flower, September 10, 2019, https://blog.littleflower.org/prayers/pearls-of-wisdom/nature-and-st-therese.

Brennan Manning, *Ragamuffin Gospel* (Sisters, OR: Multnomah Press, 2005), 90-91.

Mother Teresa, quoted in "Mother Teresa Quotes," BrainyQuote, accessed May 30, 2020, https://www.brainyquote.com/quotes/mother_teresa_164357.

Nineteen

Margery Williams Bianco and William Nicholson, *The Velveteen Rabbit, or, How Toys Become Real* (London: Doubleday Children's, 2014), 10.

Frozen, directed by Jennifer Lee and Chris Buck (2013; Burbank, CA: Walt Disney Animation, 2014), DVD.

Twenty

Craig Groeschel, *Dangerous Prayers: Because Following Jesus Was Never Meant to Be Safe* (Grand Rapids, MI: Zondervan, 2020), 40.

Richard Rohr, *Falling Upward: A Spirituality for the Two Halves of Life* (San Francisco: Jossey-Bass, 2011), 95.

Jacques Philippe, *Interior Freedom* (New York: Scepter Publishers, 2007), 58.

Richard Rohr, *Falling Upward: A Spirituality for the Two Halves of Life* (San Francisco: Jossey-Bass, 2011), 136.

Final Thoughts

C.S. Lewis, quoted in "Quotable Quote," Goodreads, accessed May 30, 2020, https://www.goodreads.com/quotes/7601569-isn-t-it-funny-that-day-by-day-nothing-changes-but.

In Memory of

Langston Hughes and Dianne Johnson, *The Collected Works of Langston Hughes* (Columbia, MO: University of Missouri Press, 2003), 52.

On Love

Mother Teresa, *No Greater Love* (Novato, CA: New World Library, 2002),157.

Frozen 2, directed by Jennifer Lee and Chris Buck (2019; Burbank, CA: Walt Disney Animation, 2020), DVD.

On Grief

C.S. Lewis, *A Grief Observed* (New York: Harper One, n.d.), 56-57.

C.S. Lewis, *A Grief Observed* (New York: Harper One, n.d.), 3

C.S. Lewis, *A Grief Observed* (New York: Harper One, n.d.), 9-10.

On Faith

Mother Teresa, quoted in "Quotable Quote," Goodreads, accessed May 30, 2020, https://www.goodreads.com/quotes/1245621-god-has-not-called-me-to-be-successful-he-has.

Jacques Philippe, *Interior Freedom* (New York: Scepter Publishers, 2007), 15.

C.S. Lewis, *A Grief Observed* (New York: Harper One, n.d.),52.

On Process

Lysa TerKeurst, *It's Not Supposed to Be This Way: Finding Unexpected Strength When Disappointments Leave You Shattered* (Nashville: Thomas Nelson, 2018), 187.

Lysa TerKeurst, *It's Not Supposed to Be This Way: Finding Unexpected Strength When Disappointments Leave You Shattered* (Nashville: Thomas Nelson, 2018), 117.

Jacques Philippe, *Interior Freedom* (New York: Scepter Publishers, 2007), 35.

On Suffering and Healing

Lysa TerKeurst, *It's Not Supposed to Be This Way: Finding Unexpected Strength When Disappointments Leave You Shattered* (Nashville: Thomas Nelson, 2018), 103.

Richard Rohr, *Falling Upward: a Spirituality for the Two Halves of Life* (San Francisco: Jossey-Bass, 2011), 54.

Brennan Manning, *Abba's Child* (Colorado Springs, CO: NavPress, 2015),12 .

On Grace

Brennan Manning, *Ragamuffin Gospel* (Sisters, OR: Multnomah Press, 2005), 81.

Made in the USA
Columbia, SC
13 September 2020